# Moderns
## Worth Keeping

# Moderns
## Worth Keeping

# Russell Fraser

**Transaction Publishers**
New Brunswick (U.S.A.) and London (U.K.)

LEE COUNTY LIBRARY
107 Hawkins Ave.
Sanford, NC 27330

Copyright © 2005 by Transaction Publishers, New Brunswick, New Jersey.
www.transactionpub.com

All rights reserved under International and Pan-American Copyright Conventions. No part of this book may be reproduced or transmitted in any form or by any means, electronic or mechanical, including photocopy, recording, or any information storage and retrieval system, without prior permission in writing from the publisher. All inquiries should be addressed to Transaction Publishers, Rutgers—The State University, 35 Berrue Circle, Piscataway, New Jersey 08854-8042.

This book is printed on acid-free paper that meets the American National Standard for Permanence of Paper for Printed Library Materials.

Library of Congress Catalog Number: 2005043700
ISBN: 0-7658-0284-8
Printed in the United States of America

Library of Congress Cataloging-in-Publication Data

Fraser, Russell A.
    Moderns worth keeping / Russell Fraser.
        p. cm.
    Includes index.
    ISBN 0-7658-0284-8 (alk. paper)
        1. Literature, Modern—20th century—History and criticism.
    2. Authors—20th century—Biography.  I. Title.


PN771.F735 2005
809'.04—dc22
[B]

2005043700

LEE COUNTY LIBRARY
107 Hawkins Ave.
Sanford, NC 27330

For George Core
Man of Letters and Friend

# Contents

# Preface

Modern times are my times, the twentieth century, and all the writers gathered here fall within it. Though they are moderns, not all are Modernist, an umbrella term for devotees of the unconscious, the irrational, and whatever is aggressively new. Amis in England was anti "all that," so was Dickey in America. But like the others in this book, both were engaged in a common endeavor, the struggle with words at their most expressive pitch. All wrote from the conviction that art speaks to the souls of men about what it means to be human.

They don't make a pantheon, nor is the table of contents meant to be exclusive. I have written elsewhere on other modern writers, and there are those I admire about whom I find I have nothing to say. Everyone on my list merits attention, however. Some haven't had their due of it, a fault I hope to redress.

A number were friends of mine, lucky for me. But I have known most of them, though not face to face, for a long time. I began to write about them early, trying to nail down their special quality. Almost all were outsiders, carrying a secret wisdom inside themselves and blurting it out to the scandal of many. This upset the applecart, and some liked doing that. Not all were nice people. (Priests may be in a state of sin without impairing their priestly function). They drank too much, but Brown was a drinking man's drinker. Amis enjoyed provoking outrage, Schwartz went crazy. Embarrassing his friends, Tate campaigned for the Nobel Prize. Had he got it, that wouldn't have been amiss.

To be ignored is the worst privation a writer can endure, and many outlived their fame. They went unread in their last days, or couldn't get published. Nonetheless, they kept writing while they had breath to do that. Warren and Fergusson are painful subjects at the end, like Synge in his different way, ravaged by disease.

Mandelstam, a casualty of the Gulag, is among the worst stories of my terrible century. But he and the others help redeem it.

Being modern, they are often hard going, niggling in their discriminations, cryptic, allusive, "elitist." Valéry wanted no such readers as he could teach. Montale, a hermetic poet, hid himself among the stuff. Muir, a prophet without honor in his own country, lived in exile. Too good a patriot, he couldn't live at home. Blackmur, who sought desperately to set the truth in relief, knew that the unambiguous truth is a fiction. Necessarily he failed in his critic's job of work, and that was the expense of greatness.

Wilde, who died as the century began, comes first on my list, but more than chronology assures him his place. New Criticism, the chief critical movement of modern times, looks back to Oscar, its Voice Crying in the Wilderness. Distinguished criticism is a specialty of the twentieth century, not surprisingly. In the vexed relation of form and content, moderns, the best of them, understood that the last term depends on the first. This understanding, though not new precisely, begins to swell in modern times. Fewer than half of my writers are primarily critics, but most have the critical gift.

Form in our postmodern time gets a bad press, many making it synonymous with stiff-neckedness. But while it reins us in, it doesn't repress us. On the contrary, it frees us, or it allows of the chance. Dancing is a formal activity and those move easiest who have learned to dance, says an old poet. Our neck grows more supple as we fit it to the yoke. For writers, the shape of the yoke is important, determining what they can tell us. Another way to put this is to say that form, the carrier of content, pervades it.

Form is structure and inevitably a purview, like the net the lepidopterist throws over his butterflies. The imperial intelligence, craving a total view, will always seek to transcend it. Moderns I call worth keeping are more equable or possibly only parochial, lacking a head for abstraction. Valéry hunted the abstract truth all his life, hoping to breathe a purer ether than ours. But he fell on his own reality, a phrase of Blackmur's, and his greatest poem turns away from abstraction to honor the body and its claims. No critic is more insistently lower case than Warren, no playwright more earthbound than Synge, "that rooted man," no poet more entangled in particulars than Dickey. Each writes above his lintel the line from St. John's Gospel: "In the beginning was the word."

Truth not being apparent, blazing in the heavens like the sign that showed itself to the Emperor Constantine, they come at it by exploring words and their latencies. The big picture is beyond them—Mandelstam would like to have painted it but couldn't—so they render life piecemeal, modifying what they see or locating it in a how, when, or where phrase. Or they compare one thing to another or present one thing in terms of another, the closest they can get to its likeness. Growing practiced in this activity, they acquire a voice that sets them apart. Each is a notable stylist, recognizably himself, and given to obiter dicta. Our postmodern time, believing in a naked truth or no truth, doesn't think that a reason to praise them.

I find it significant that they needed to write poems. This need varies in intensity, sometimes petering out in youth, and the level of competence does too. But they have in common the sense that poetry is our most nearly adequate response to experience, not least when the experience bedevils us or lifts us up to the skies. More than personal friendship or social or political allegiance, this sense links them together. Even Austin Warren, essentially a prose stylist, wrote poems as a young man. He called them "eclectic," work of a gifted student, the characterization telling of his arrogance and his humility. If you meant to write poetry you had to be a maitre, otherwise what was the point?

Writing about poetry, though a lesser activity, has its requirements too. First of all, the critic must be immediately involved with the language the poet uses, not a paraphrase of it but the very words, including the way they should sound and the connotations that trail after them. I learned Russian in the sixties when I went to the Soviet Union to help negotiate the academic exchange, but what I learned then I have largely forgotten. And this disables me from criticizing Mandelstam the poet. His prose is another matter, and though hardly common coin, is substantially accessible in English.

Earlier versions of my chapters appeared in the *Nation*, the *Southern Review*, *Sewanee Review*, *Michigan Quarterly Review*, *New Republic*, and *Sulfur*, and in books from Houghton Mifflin and the University of Michigan Press. My thanks to the editors and publishers. Each chapter has been revised, in some cases rewritten. The first time round I didn't get it quite right, and am glad to have another crack at the subject.

*Russell Fraser*
*Ann Arbor and Honolulu*

# 1

## Revenge on Oscar Wilde

Among moderns worth keeping, Wilde just makes the cut, dying as the twentieth century began. Though much of him is inferior, a pastiche of other men's trademark successes, he had one astonishing success of his own, and this is another reason he makes it. Modern criticism sets him higher, alleging his moral and ethical side. Ellmann's humdrum biography, the standard account, presents a serious social critic. But though his art is often earnest, serious it isn't. Sometimes, however, he merits our praise, even to the nth power, and this side of him mustn't be missed.

For both his detractors and idolaters he dramatizes an enduring cliché, the alien genius at odds with society. Scandalized by his novel *The Picture of Dorian Gray*, a contemporary thought its opinions would land their author up "at Bow Street," step one on the road to Reading Gaol. Wilde made sure this happened. The homosexuality he flaunted outraged his own time but our time perceives it as a badge of honor. It thinks that hypocritical prejudice, not ours, the Victorians', made him a victim because he wasn't like everybody else. Oddly, he accepted this view of himself. Prison wasn't the worst thing that befell him.

The most intelligent man of his time, he violated his intelligence, rejecting what he knew in favor of conventional half-truths. Having no substantial self, he assumed roles, Melmoth the Wanderer, Marsyas the satyr, flayed alive by the god, even St. Francis of Assisi. You could say the same of Shakespeare, but his roles are immortal, Wilde's appropriate to farce. Degas said he had the air of playing Byron in a suburban theater. His homosexuality wasn't "Greek," his synonym for all things beautiful, but lurid and promiscuous, telling of a man who never grew up. Self-pity consumed him, viti-ating his taste. Guido Reni's morbid St. Sebastian, the patron saint of homosexuals and a favorite of his, suits the self-anointed martyr. At the end of his life he took for his alias the name of the "lovely brown boy" with the "crisp, clustering hair and red lips." Never mind the morality: this is at least bathetic.

But his brief time in the sun guaranteed him immortality, whether or not he deserved it. He lives to the future as the master spirit of the Nineties, the ancestral homeland of those who give first place to the word. Unlike his second-rate cronies, men of the Yellow Nine-ties, he knew that "All bad poetry comes from genuine feeling," or rather one side of him knew this. It's what's up front that counts, he might have told us, and did tell us that only shallow people don't judge by appearances. (Shallow people think he was having them on.) His chief argument against Christianity was the demotic style of St. Paul. You had to have a heart of stone to read the death of Little Nell without laughing.

Two great but flawed contemporaries, Ruskin and Pater, put their stamp on his genius. Ruskin boosted the claims of the medieval gothic style (as he understood it) over that of the Renaissance. Blame him for the proliferating of bastard gothic, especially on college campuses in the United States. Wilde identified the gothic style with suffering and denial, and the style of the Renaissance with affirma-tion and joy. He was on the side of joy. But his work—notably the last pages of *The Picture of Dorian Gray*—promotes the gloomy idea that suffering, expiation, and atonement are good for the soul. This suggestion of the masochistic offers a key to his achievement.

Ruskin plays into the achievement not only as a propagandist for art but for Socialism, not theoretical but passionate, not Marxist but artistic. The protest of the artist, who is the great economist, is at heart esthetic, full of horror for ugliness and waste. In *The Crown of Wild Olive*, a moving attack on the acquisitive society, Ruskin converted Wilde to Socialism. But Wilde's Socialism, unlike Ruskin's, was inspired as much by his distaste for the million as it was by fellow feeling for the poor.

At Oxford, where he heard Ruskin lecture, he met Walter Pater, a sedate Oxford don. Wilde of the green carnation is the final em-bodiment of the doctrine of art for art's sake that Pater only wrote about. In the conclusion to *The Renaissance*, for instance: "Not the fruit of experience, but experience itself, is the end. A counted number of pulses only is given to us." The thing is to savor them, living a life of perpetual intoxication. Art is like cayenne pepper on the tongue, or like curious forms of sexual play and sexual perversity; or it is like crime, because criminals, more than other men, explore the arcane and forbidden; or, finally, art is like punishment, inflicting exquisite sensations of pain. That is Pater carried to his logical conclusion. Wilde acted it out in his life.

The borrower at random of other men's ill-assorted ideas, he is the type of the pack-rat personality. Until his last decade, he had never done anything of genuine account. He was famous or infamous, and yet he was negligible. A hundred years later, there seems little to talk about. And then suddenly, in his late thirties, this brightly colored moth produced *The Importance of Being Earnest*, as near perfection as man's work can be.

In the year he finished it, his world fell to pieces. He spent two years in prison, coming out broken in body and spirit. He went to the Continent to live for three years more, in exile and squalor, under the romantic name Sebastian Melmoth. On the 30th of November, 1900, he died in a cheap Paris hotel. The work is more interesting and more important than the life on Wilde's own principle that "Good artists exist simply in what they make, and consequently are perfectly uninteresting in what they are." Everything he made that outlives him is confined to four years of intense creative activity early in the 1890s: an ambitious political essay, "The Soul of Man Under Socialism" (1891); a disagreeable but brilliant novel, *The Picture of Dorian Gray* (1891); a hothouse tragedy, *Salome* (1893), written in French, translated by his lover, Lord Alfred Douglas; and four comedies, the last of which, given its kind, is without a rival in the history of English drama. That sounds like wild hyperbole but wait.

\* \* \*

In the three lesser comedies, *Lady Windermere's Fan* (1892), *A Woman of No Importance* (1893), and *An Ideal Husband* (1895), Ibsen is the "unseen good old man behind the arras." But this is only to speak of influence, superficial at that, and each of these plays is filtered through and colored by the vulgar personality of

Sir Arthur Wing Pinero. Bringing up the rear, *The Importance of Being Earnest* (1895) stands Pinero on his head. Turning the well-made play inside out, it sends up its stock conventions the way Fats Waller sends up Tin Pan Alley or Mae West the Babylonish woman. It isn't simply the best of Wilde but his antithesis. The work that precedes it will show this.

I look at the poetry first because Wilde, in his own time, figured as a poet of pretension. He isn't much of a poet, though Ellmann's judgment of *The Ballad of Reading Gaol* is probably right: "Once read, it is never forgotten." Now that time has sifted the poems, they take their natural place in *The Yellow Book*, about on a par with Symons, Dowson, Beardsley, and Lionel Johnson who, as Pound remembered him, died

> By falling from a high stool in a pub ...
> But showed no trace of alcohol
> At the autopsy, privately performed—
> Tissue preserved—The pure mind
> Arose toward Newman as the whiskey warmed.

Hypothetically wicked, the poetry is marred, said Arthur Symons, by "a desperate and ineffectual attempt to get into key with the Latin Quarter." He and his companions of the Cheshire Cheese weren't really there, though. They were in London, conning other men's books. You keep hearing behind Wilde's music the attenuated music of Arnold, Swinburne, Tennyson, others. Even the inevitable anthology piece, *The Ballad of Reading Gaol* (1898), though founded on personal experience, reminds you not so much of itself as *The Rime of the Ancient Mariner*. The red shirt Wilde wears on his socialist side is worn mostly for the color's sake. His classicism is a refuge from the dust and soil of the present, his romanticism is "Wardour Street," like the fake Celtic antiquity Yeats's early poems are dipped in.

But Yeats, getting older, threw away the sword upstairs. A sonnet of Wilde's on the sale of Keats's letters gets at the difference between them:

> Is it not said that many years ago,
>   In a far Eastern town, some soldiers ran
>   With torches through the midnight, and began

To wrangle for mere raiment, and to throw
Dice for the garments of a wretched man?

These lines of Wilde's quickened in Yeats's memory when he wrote about Synge and the Playboy ("Once when midnight smote the air,/ Eunuchs ran through Hell and met/ On every crowded street to stare"), again years later in a prayer for his son ("And when through all the town there ran/ The servants of Your enemy"). But the reminiscence is only a taking off point, and what Yeats does with the hints afforded him is like Mozart improvising on Salieri.

Wilde's poems are made of paste and he judged them: "In a very ugly and sensible age, the arts borrow, not from life, but from each other" (*Pen, Pencil, and Poison*). His work, as Yeats said of the early work of Synge, is only a mirror reflecting a mirror. It could hardly be anything else, given Wilde's legacy as one of the myriad begot by Descartes upon Calvin. His legacy denied him the chance of getting at truth, neither the truth at the bottom of the well nor that humbler kind that is at least itself. It left him with imitation and sensation: art as mimicry, art as visceral tickling.

The mysteries of Catholicism stirred him in his viscera. He liked the smell of incense, the vestments, the pageantry, the Latinity. Rumor says that his Dorian Gray is about to join the Church: "He loved to kneel down on the cold marble pavement, and watch the priest, in his stiff flowered dalmatic, slowly and with white hands moving aside the veil of the tabernacle, or raising aloft the jewelled lantern-shaped monstrance." Sensation abstracted from its context and snuffed up for its own sake attracts this writer and his hero. It isn't surprising that on his deathbed he turned Catholic. The conversion gave his life the point and symmetry of art—the lesser kind that loves and dwells on and seeks to reproduce sounds and colors and smells: art for art's sake or the sake of a tickle.

Like other modern writers cut off from their "material sap" (the phrase is Shakespeare's and asks us to see a tree, its branches severed from the trunk), Wilde mines discrete details. They don't modify or qualify but are stitched to a backcloth. Dorian Gray studies perfumes and sniffs "burning odorous gums from the East." He loves "curious" music: "grinning Negroes beating monotonously upon copper drums." He loves jewels and embroideries, and appears at a ball in a dress covered with 560 pearls. In *Salome*, the interest isn't so much in the story as in the special effects. When John the Baptist, who has been sitting at the bottom of a well, is beheaded by a giant Negro, "a huge black arm, the arm of the Executioner, comes forth from the cistern, bearing on a silver shield the head of Iokanaan." Salome seizes the head and kisses the gory lips. Wilde wanted that black arm against that silver shield, he wanted the bleeding head posed against the half-naked girl: color, contrast, oxymoron. Even in the comedies the impulse is painterly, "A work of art, on the whole, but showing the influence of too many schools."

Stealing from one play, Wilde enriched the next. Like Lord Henry Wotton in the novel, he would have sacrificed his birthright for the sake of an epigram. This artist-without-a-conscience had no governing idea. Like other young men with their head in the clouds, he courted the tragic muse. Shaw said he was too susceptible to "fine art" not to have begun "with a strenuous imitation of a great dramatic poem, Greek or Shakespearean." Of course his tragedies are sound and fury. He is one of that vast company who dominate the English drama from the later seventeenth century almost to the present—playwrights who know nothing of experience, of the world outside the ego, and for whom the greater world has come more and more to resemble catena. As for the connected chain, its nature, even its existence, elude apprehension. He is the playwright as Faulkner's Benjy Compson, moving through embalmed darkness.

One of the sons of Pater, he believed that "on this short day of frost and sun" we can really know nothing. Experience, meaning only "a group of impressions," is ringed round for each of us by a thick wall of personality no voice has ever pierced. Like solitary prisoners we dream our world, only conjecturing what lies outside the cell that confines us. This paraphrase of Pater gives the state of mind that destroyed the drama after the Renaissance. "The intellect," says one of Wilde's characters, a mouthpiece, "is not a serious thing, and never has been. It is an instrument on which one plays, that is all." All thought is immoral, its essence destruction. "If you think of anything, you kill it. Nothing survives being thought of." The definition of life is "a bad quarter of an hour made up of exquisite moments."

\*   \*   \*

But the same nineteenth century that diminished Wilde retrieved him. Denying the claims of intellect, it culminated in solipsism, but in the same century intellect begins to be honored again. This is the subject of somebody's else's great book, not yet written. Among its protagonists are Marx, the Schoolman as philosopher, and Ibsen, the Schoolman as playwright. Wilde, who would have paled at one and snickered at the other, follows in the footsteps of both.

In his three lesser comedies, he set out to grapple with the nature of experience. The first of them, *Lady Windermere's Fan*, opens with the young heroine on her twenty-first birthday. The coming of age is of course symbolic. Lady Windermere, in the beginning, calls herself a Puritan. Allowing no compromise, she will have no truck with anyone whose skirts are soiled. The cruel question she puts to the fallen woman Mrs. Erlynne, who unbeknownst to her is her own mother: "What have I to do with you?" is the central question of a serious play. At the end of the play, Lady Windermere discovers that "I" and "you" have much to do with each other, that the world is the same for all of us, and "good and evil, sin and innocence, go through it hand in hand." If you believe the playwright, Lady Windermere's eyes are opened.

In the second comedy, *A Woman of No Importance*, another young Puritan, Hester Worsley, dares say, "Let all women who have sinned be punished," and even, "The sins of the parents should be visited on the children." The same central question comes up again, put this time by the fallen woman Mrs. Arbuthnot: "What have women who have not sinned to do with me, or I with them?" The answer is "Everything." Puritan and fallen woman embrace, and the Puritan says humbly, "I was wrong. God's law is . . . Love."

*An Ideal Husband*, third among the comedies, sticks close to the formula. Lady Chiltern declines to forgive anyone who has ever done a shameful thing. Idealizing her husband Sir Robert as a paragon, she insists that "a person who has once been guilty of a dishonest and dishonorable action... should be shunned." "Would you apply that rule to everyone?" asks the very dishonest Mrs. Cheveley. And Lady Chiltern answers, "Yes, to everyone, without exception." In this play-world ironies are patent, and it isn't surprising to learn that the ideal husband has built his fortune by selling a government secret. Mrs. Cheveley knows what he has done. So the heroine's question: "What has my husband to do . . . with a

woman like you?"—the same question raised in the earlier comedies—has an answer we have learned to expect. The plot of the
play becomes the changing of Lady Chiltern, her ultimate discov-
ery that "Nobody is incapable of doing a foolish thing. Nobody is
incapable of doing a wrong thing."

Wilde's three plays deal with material that is as serious as Ibsen's
later dramas of reconciliation and forgiveness. The comparison ends
there, though, and the seriousness in each is only pretending. Form
is the great culprit, where the content is what the form makes it. The
content looks like Ibsen but the technique is that of Scribe and Sardou
and Pinero, makers of the well-made play. It colors the content,
jaundiced, hectic, bilious, or pretty pink, as the form decides.

The real protagonist of *Lady Windermere's Fan* isn't Mrs. Erlynne
or her daughter, but her daughter's fan. Writing letters and misplac-
ing them—like Paula Tanqueray in Pinero's mock-serious play—is
the hinge the plot turns on. Lady Windermere has written what she
calls, "That fatal letter!" And so has Mrs. Arbuthnot in *A Woman of
No Importance*. And so has her son Gerald. Lord Illingworth, the
heavy, finds Gerald's letter, as he has already found the mother's.
Reading it provokes the crisis and resolution of the play. When
Desdemona drops the handkerchief, is that the real hinge of Othello?
Some, anticipating Wilde, think it is.

In *An Ideal Husband*, the letter writing goes on. Sir Robert, the
pretended paragon who has revealed a state secret in writing, had
thought the incriminating letter destroyed. There wouldn't be a play
if it had, though. Sir Robert's wife, the Puritan Lady Chiltern, writes
a damaging letter too. And it also falls into the hands of a scoun-
drel, preparing the crisis of the play and the Puritan's conversion.
But how to get these letters back from the villain? Wilde's answer is
to let her drop a diamond brooch she'd stolen years ago, and let the
hero find it—and blackmail the blackmailing villain.

We know what happens when oil and water mix, and the intru-
sion of the fortuitous in a realistic play is like that. All Wilde's comedies are indebted to the new technical realism. All honor the uni-
ties. The action, twenty-four hours' worth, takes place in familiar
venues, a drawing room or a gentleman's flat. No pains are spared
to convey the illusion of reality on stage. All this looks like life. But
then the playwright thrusts into his lifelike frame the un-lifelike
conventions of farce. (Nothing wrong with farce if taken neat.) He

makes a conundrum the centerpiece of his play, like Lady Windermere's question, "Who is this woman?" He allows his characters to meet accidentally, after many years' separation, as Mrs. Arbuthnot meets Lord Illingworth, her former lover, in *A Woman of No Importance*, and as Lady Chiltern meets her schoolgirl enemy, Mrs. Cheveley, in *An Ideal Husband*: "[*Advances toward Mrs. Cheveley with a sweet smile. Then suddenly stops, and bows rather distantly.*] I think Mrs. Cheveley and I have met before."

Characters whisk in and out of the verisimilar setting, hiding behind curtains (*Lady Windermere's Fan*), or pilfering a letter when no one is looking (*An Ideal Husband*). You can get away with that in *Twelfth Night* because the play is romantic comedy, not simpleminded but obeying different rules. What you can't do is insist on realism, and stuff it with the conventions of romance. Smile if you make your hero Japhet a Foundling in Search of a Father, the bread and butter of English melodrama from the seventeenth century on. For example, Sir Richard Steele of the Addison & Steele firm in his Conscious Lovers, Edward Moore in *The Foundling*, Richard Cumberland in *The* West Indian. Colley Cibber's *Love's Last Shift*, shaking up the basic ingredients, has a husband who doesn't recognize the woman he's married. Incredibly, Wilde belongs in this company.

He has the formula down pat in *Lady Windermere's Fan*, whose heroine is an orphan in search of a mother. Step by step, Gerald Arbuthnot, in *A Woman of No Importance*, is an orphan in search of a father. The scene in which he finds his father is surely one of the funniest in the repertory, bad luck for the play. The best comment on this pretending to seriousness is parody, and the best parody I know is the mid-nineteenth century farce, *Box and Cox*. In Cibber's sentimental comedy, *Love's Last Shift*, the identity of the wife is established when she shows her husband his name, tattooed on her arm—the one detail Wilde omits in *A Woman of No Importance*. But Box and Cox remembers:

> BOX: Cox! You'll excuse the apparent insanity of the remark, but the more I gaze on your features, the more I'm convinced that you're my long-lost brother.
> BOX. The very observation I was going to make to you.
> COX: Ah—tell me—in mercy tell me—have you such a thing as a strawberry mark on your left arm?

COX. No!
BOX. Then 'tis he! [*They rush into each other's arms.*]

* * *

But *The Importance of Being Earnest* is more than a parody of hokum. It effects a metamorphosis, true of all considerable art. "Those are pearls that were his eyes" is the rubric. For instance:

JACK. I have lost both my parents.
LADY BRACKNELL. *Both?*.... That seems like carelessness.

The rejoinder, more than inconsequent, literally incendiary, burns a hole in the pseudo-serious play. Wilde managed that only once, technique and what it says about him tripping him up elsewhere. He wasn't of enough size to break free from the murk that swirled around perception in his time. He didn't have enough substance to "expatiate and confer," like Milton's philosopher-bees. He lacked character, different from talent.

His technique is a lie because it expresses his own limited perception, when he wears his serious hat, of the nature of social intercourse. The psychology of supposedly good characters in his plays is so overblown as to demand the grossly melodramatic plot. Plot is the dramatist's way of testing his thesis, and "thesis" is another way of saying "vision of life." The play is deformed because the playwright is purblind. But in *The Importance of Being Earnest* he gets rid of his singing robes. Though raising questions, he doesn't plague us with answers. Lady Bracknell doesn't come round in the end, self-convicted of her snobbery, etc. She isn't a character to be converted but a target to shoot at. On that limited ground, she overwhelms us.

Bernard Shaw dismissed *The Importance of Being Earnest* because it fails to get beyond obiter dicta. The play had to be apprentice work, it being "almost inhuman." Shaw's objection does credit to his humanity. But characters in *The Importance of Being Earnest* aren't supposed to bleed, if you prick them. Unlike Don Quixote, they have no "hold on our sympathy." Wilde knew better than to let them get one.

Absent the heart-warming power and we are thrown back, says Shaw regretfully, on the force and delicacy of the wit. Meant in reprobation, that stabs the heart of Wilde's achievement. His super-ficial-seeming commentary on marriage and class, literature and morality, skewers convention's low-level view of these subjects, every one of them big game. Some examples:

> CECILY. They have been eating muffins. That looks like repentance.
>
> LADY BRACKNELL. I was obliged to call on dear Lady Harbury. I haven't been there since her poor husband's death. I never saw a woman so altered; she looks quite twenty years younger.
>
> ALGERNON: I hear her hair has turned quite gold from grief.
>
> MISS PRISM: The good end happily, and the bad unhappily. That is what Fiction means.
>
> CECILY: When I see a spade I call it a spade.
>
> GWENDOLEN: I am glad to say I have never seen a spade.

*   *   *

Before going up to Oxford, Wilde studied classics at Dublin's Trinity College. TCD was William Congreve's school, and the pairing of these two is suggestive. Wilde is Congreve redivivus, a "superficial" writer whose truths are all up front. Gifted with a genius for knocking down shoddy structures, he is only middling at building good ones. In *An Ideal Husband*, Mrs. Cheveley is asked: "You prefer to be natural?" And she answers: "Sometimes. But it is such a very difficult pose to keep up." This answer—every American ought to write it over his lintel—exposes the fraudulent reading of human nature that created the natural man, a fixture in the theater from Cumberland to Boucicault—to Wilde.

Trying to present the natural man, Wilde isn't up to more than cliché. Lord Goring, who puts the question to Mrs. Cheveley, is an elegant dandy with a heart of gold. Faithful to his cliché side, he tries to soften the Puritanical hardness of Lady Chiltern: "Life," he says, "cannot be understood without much charity, cannot be lived without much charity." That is an unexceptionable saying. Here is Goring saying the same thing, but transmuted: "It is the growth of the moral sense in woman that makes marriage such a hopeless, one-sided institution." The flippancy demolishes a lie, and this is Wilde's immaculate achievement.

But his soberly said truths are only sober. A grieving mother makes the real Oscar laugh: "We always fancy that when . . . [our children] come to man's estate and know us better, they will repay us. But it is not so. The world draws them from our side . . . and they are unjust to us often, for when they find life bitter they blame us for it, and when they find it sweet we do not taste its sweetness with them." But apothegmatic Wilde is an artist: "Children begin by loving their parents. After a time they judge them. Rarely, if ever, do they forgive them."

When he tries for the old Shakespeherian Rag, he writes *Salome*. His sentiment is sentimentality (the famous fairy tale *The Happy Prince*, or the final scene of *A Woman of No Importance*). The problems he sets himself in his plays are fictitious. How seriously can we take a play which turns on a woman's desire to make her way back into society (*Lady Windermere's Fan*)? Can we believe in a heroine who thinks the sins of the parents should be visited on the children? Or in the struggles of a hero to make his mother marry his father (*A Woman of No Importance*)? If a wife tells her husband that any taint of dishonor will write finis to their marriage, do we want to stick around for the ending (*An Ideal Husband*)?

No problems, only parlor games. No people, either. Wilde can't envisage real people. The nineteenth century produced many like him, though few of his stature, writers who can't tell their heroes from their villains. Thackeray is one, and Charlotte Brontë thought him a cynic. What would she have made of Wilde? But Thackeray, like Wilde, faces both ways, and mingled with the mockery is a strain of moral earnestness, warring against it. In his best novel, he runs with the hares but hunts with the respectable hounds. His official heroine is a little pink-faced chit, but his real heroine Becky Sharpe must fail because she is clever. The same confusion runs all but the last of Wilde's plays on the rocks. Henry James mirrors it in Washington Square when Mrs. Penniman asks her brother Dr. Sloper: "Do you think it better to be clever than good?" "Good for what?" he answers. Wilde is mordant Dr. Sloper and his sentimental sister in one.

His attractive characters, who speak for the joy of life, are felt as walking the primrose path. Though they are given the good and bright and right things to say, they are always put down by the dowdies. Lord Darlington is much the best character in *Lady*

*Windermere's Fan*. People, he observes, are either charming or tedious. He takes the side of the charming. He is one of the charming people himself. And the point of view he speaks for—the abhorrence of self-righteousness—is the one Lady Windermere veers round to. But in the meantime poor Darlington has become the vile seducer of melodrama. He has taken to praising stiff-necked Lady W. as the only good woman he's known. What has happened to his sunny disposition? Wilde, in part a Puritan himself, has begun to suspect it. The same disquieting betrayal by the author awaits his one intelligent character in *A Woman of No Importance*. Lord Illingworth is the only possible hero. Wilde makes him the villain. The same fate awaits Lord Henry Wotton, the real hero of *The Picture of Dorian Gray*. But we remember him long after we have forgotten Lady Windermere and Mrs. Arbuthnot and that tiresome gigolo Dorian Gray.

But Wilde feared the singularity in his elegant purveyors of wit. He believed in his heart, with one of the characters in his novel, that "It is better not to be different from one's fellows," and that "The ugly and the stupid have the best of it in this world." In the end, he gave them the best of it. He believed that an ignorant dairymaid has more to her than a man of the world. "She knew nothing, but she had everything that he had lost." That is poppycock, and the time's revenge on Wilde is that he came to endorse it.

He, the cleverest man in England, wanted us to suppose that cleverness outsmarts itself, that cleverness kills love, that "There is more to be said for stupidity than people imagine." The emancipated man, a connoisseur of experience, who was shrewd enough to see that "It is the people who don't know how to play with . . . [fire] who get burned," was fatuous enough to say that "Too much experience is a dangerous thing." He wasn't so much a paradox as an animated confusion, at war with himself and incapable of knowing his mind. The Renaissance enthusiasm and the Gothic austerity, Pater and Ruskin, were forever tugging away inside him. Constant warfare, never resolved, it made for equivocal plays.

Pinero aims at the mark and misses, showing us by default how to score. In The Second Mrs. Tanqueray, marriage "is such a beautiful thing . . . and if people in our position don't respect it, and set a good example by living happily with their husbands, what can you expect from the middle classes?" Wilde thinks that over, then picks up his pen. Algernon is speaking of his servant: "Lane's views on marriage seem somewhat lax. Really, if the lower orders don't set us a good example, what on earth is the use of them? They seem, as a class, to have absolutely no sense of moral responsibility."

Wilde, like Shakespeare, makes us mind true things by their mockeries, a phrase from the history plays where truth and its simulacra jostle for place. The 1890s, the decade Wilde triumphed in, saw the founding of the Labor Party. Keir Hardie, its first leader, had a world of goodness in him and deserves to be remembered far more than Wilde. As to desert, though! Time, intolerant of goodness, "worships language and forgives Everyone by whom it lives." It is language that insures Wilde's survival.

However jejune his earlier comedies, something in each of them sticks to our ribs. In *A Woman of No Importance*, two characters are talking in the garden of a country house:

> LORD ILLINGWORTH. Shall we go in to tea?
> MRS. ALLONBY. Do you like such simple pleasures?
> LORD ILLINGWORTH. I adore simple pleasures. They are the last refuge of the complex. But, if you wish, let us stay here. . . . The Book of Life begins with a man and a woman in a garden.
> MRS. ALLONBY. It ends with Revelations.
> LORD ILLINGWORTH. You fence divinely. But the button has come off your foil.
> MRS. ALLONBY. I have still the mask.
> LORD ILLINGWORTH. It makes your eyes lovelier.

Reading or listening to an interchange like that, we are carried back to Shakespeare's elegant comedies of sexual contention, *Love's Labor's Lost* and *Much Ado About Nothing*. Wilde sought to return to the high artifice of the drama in its salad days: stichomythia, the poetry of wit. He worked his magic only off and on, failing to transcend the world he was born into. But I think we enlist him, in his best and highest moments, in the company of Shakespeare and Congreve.

# 2

# J. M. Synge's Magic Mirror

Synge's death in his thirties is terrible to contemplate. A passionate sensual man, like that Petrarch he translated, he was in love with the actress Molly Allgood, and just then coming into his force. She played his heroines at the Abbey Theater, and he wrote that the two of them made God jealous. "The time was coming," his Petrarch says, "when Love and Decency can keep company." The lovers could have sat together, the artist saying out all the things in his heart. "But Death had his grudge against me."

Even so, I make out Synge's story as lucky. Like his Playboy, mounted on the springtide of the stars of luck, he had a magic flowering in his last years, roughly 1903-1909. In this time he wrote the two one-acters, *In the Shadow of the Glen* and *Riders to the Sea*, the partly comic, partly tragic plays, *The Well of the Saints* and *The Playboy of the Western World*, a single farce, *The Tinker's Wedding*, and the final unfinished tragedy, *Deirdre of the Sorrows*. His genius, welling up suddenly, then quenched, is like Keats's, unlike Mozart's, who was already strangling serpents in his cradle. Had Synge died a few years earlier, he would have left a scattering of reviews and articles, a bad play, and an unpublishable book. His early work, in Yeats's words, was "full of that kind of morbidity that has its root in too much brooding over methods of expression, and ways of looking upon life, which come, not out of life but out of literature, images reflected from mirror to mirror." But turning away from books, he held the mirror up to nature.

Beware this well-worn truism, though. Hamlet's advice to the players has to be looked at twice, like all the familiar quotations, and neither Synge nor Shakespeare is a naturalist in theater. For both, the natural world is seen through a crazy glass, as when we hear that the Playboy has left his dead father rotting in the grave, without a Christian to drink a drop in his memory. Synge's publican, who wants a wake, has a better scenario. Throw the body on the crupper of a Kerry mule, he says, and drive him westwards "like holy Joseph in the days gone by." We are past this amazing similitude that likens a squatter's funeral to the Flight into Egypt before we slam on the brakes and look back.

Synge, swarthy as a gypsy, exotic, verging on sinister, is like that Jew-man Pegeen Mike in the play hopes to marry. He has ten kegs of gold in the attic. James Sleator did his likeness and it hangs on my study wall. Friends ask about this "Man of the West," perhaps a revolutionary whose name eludes them: did he storm the Winter Palace or fight on the barricades with the French Communards? Revolutionary in his core, though not a fighter for causes, he did something better. He recreated tragedy. He is head and shoulders above contemporaries like Lloyd George, the first Roosevelt, and Lenin. Synge and Orville Wright were born the same year, 1876. But the Wright brothers only created an airplane.

The connection between Synge's ending and his beginning is mysterious, like the course of that fabulous river, the Arethusa, that rises in one place, goes underground, and surfaces again in another. Somewhere in the middle is a revelation. By nature it isn't open to rationalizing, and though Synge's biographers have served him well, a cause-and-effect biography is unlikely to be written. How do you explain metamorphosis? My best analogy is to St. Paul on the road to Damascus.

All great drama is rooted in its time, and is both popular and social. The description is valid for Synge. But he isn't like his medieval predecessors, the masters of the morality and mystery, communal, whatever else, and he isn't like those Elizabethan playwrights whose excellence comes partly from collaborating with the crowd in the pit. Though it is proper to speak of him in the same breath as Shakespeare, a comparison worth anything will highlight their difference. Shakespeare couldn't have been clubbable, never that, but traditions abound of his amiable side. One has him drinking with cronies at "a certain public house in the neighborhood of Stratford." Doubtless this was part of the mask he wore, but at least he cared to wear it. Synge said he grew to young manhood without conversing with a single man or woman whose opinions he shared. Beside Shakespeare, he looks almost naked.

He came from an Evangelical Protestant family in a land of Roman Catholics. His early training reflected the embittered zeal of the minister who was his maternal grandfather, and who spent his whole career "in the bush," fighting the barbarians of Catholic Cork. As he got older, he became a rebel, unlike Shakespeare, steady as she goes. "By the time I was 16 or 17," he wrote, "I had renounced Christianity after a good deal of wobbling." So he opened a chasm between his present and past, "and between myself and my kindred and friends."

His membership in the Ascendancy class made him non grata to professional Irish. Cyril Cusack, who played Christy Mahon at the Abbey, suggested bizarrely that his ideal audience was Parisian. The hatred his class inspired turned the countryside into a place of terror. Twigs in Ireland became a fasces, raised to smite the oppressor. There were times, said Lady Gregory, that she didn't sit between the lamp and the window. Synge, a target of the terror, hoped to be righteous, and his brother Edward's wringing of the peasantry drove him to protest. His mother knew better, retorting simply, "What would become of us if our tenants in Galway stopped paying their rents?"

You can answer the question in more than one way. Parnell, becoming a traitor to his class, answered by making war against the source of his income. Synge thought about it, then retreated to Paris. At a public lecture there, having heard the anarchist Sebastian Faure, he wrote in his diary, "*tres interessant mais fou.*" In 1892, when the Irish National Literary Society held its first meeting in Dublin, with Yeats and Maud Gonne as featured speakers, Synge was off in Wicklow for the summer. He lived in a boycotted house, protected by the police.

Fifteen years later, the police come into the story again. The opening of the *Playboy* set off a riot, and this time they protected the actors from the mob. A parallel with a difference, it gives a measure of the distance Synge traveled.

Poor health and the pirate's look that will have scared away children aggravated his apartness. He didn't want to inflict his sickness on anybody else, so decided when still a boy not to marry. He couldn't do sports but became a great walker. He took up the violin, more pleasure for a solitary. This is how his mother saw him, still in his teens and studying for a degree at TCD, the Ascendancy school: "He leads a queer solitary life, poor boy. He plays his fiddle a great deal and reads and takes a walk. I wonder what he will turn into by and by."

Who doesn't know what he will turn into, a late nineteenth-century aesthete, Stephen Dedalus. Rejecting the life of his times—too crude, too coarse—he cultivates art but isn't able to create it. Dying unfulfilled, he is Pound's Mauberly, exhaling a minor fragrance, the perfume of the *fin de siècle*. But the revelation from Heaven singled him out from his peers. He himself felt there was that in him "of value to the world" (he said to his sweetheart), and seeking to bring it up to the light, he worked his own metamorphosis.

All the great ones are like this, Shakespeare, a new Dick Whittington, Whitman, journalist and dandy but breaking the mold, Yeats, vamping till ready in the shadow of Spenser and Shelley. Synge, like Yeats, beat his way back to solid and substantial things. He learned to repudiate "twaddle," his word: Thomas à Kempis and J. K. Huysmans, religion and the religion of art. "I will not deny my masculine existence nor rise, if I can, by facile abnegation. I despise the hermit and the monk and pity only the adulterer and the drunkard. There is one world of souls and no flesh and no devil." Acting out this credo, he breathed life into an imagined world, like ours in detail but more stylish. The souls that live in it are very tangible, and his details make a form.

\*   \*   \*

Years after Synge died of cancer, Yeats wrote how, near the end, he "chose the living world for text,"

> And never could have rested in the tomb
> But that, long traveling, he had come
> Towards nightfall upon certain set apart
> In a most desolate stony place,
> Towards nightfall upon a race
> Passionate and simple like his heart.

The place was Aran, three spits of land off the west coast of Ireland. Synge came to stay five times between 1898-1902. Mostly he stayed on Inishmaan, the middle island, "where men must reap with knives because of the stones." Wasting nothing, islanders used the stones to fence their flat fields, scoured by wind to the bedrock. The soil is artificial, clay mixed with sand and seaweed and spread to a thickness of only a few inches in cavities in the rock. Potatoes grow in this meager soil. The seas teem with fish, but most are exported to England.

On Inishmaan Synge discovered his land of heart's desire, like Edwin Muir who found another Eden in the Orkneys. Mist and pounding seas separated his island from the Connemara coast, thirty miles distant, and sometimes the natives were cut off from the mainland for weeks. In good weather the ocean is like glass, but there are days when the steamer from Galway Bay starts out and has to go back. This enforced isolation, different from Synge's alienated youth, turned out to be good for his soul.

Ruins of an old stone fort or dun loomed over his cottage. The dun was pagan and you feel its presence in his plays, layered with Christianity over a prehistoric substrate. Climbing up there, he stretched out like Christy Mahon, "the half of the day in the brown ferns with his belly to the sun." Or he looked out to sea or down on the people, a scurry of blue-flannel shirts and red petticoats. Gray is overall, though, the color of the stones in Aran's drywall fences, of the sea, and the Celtic crosses in the burial ground. The curraghs, or fishing boats, are black.

Better than competent on the violin, Synge hoped to be a concert performer but had to give it up out of shyness. On Aran, however, the shyness fell away. He was like a snake shedding its skin.

> At first I tried to play standing, but on the upward stroke my bow came in contact with the salt fish and oilskins that hung from the rafters; so I settled myself at last on a table in the corner.

Someone held his music before him, and as he began playing, "a tall man bounded out from his stool under the chimney and began flying round the kitchen." Estimating this native dancer's sure and graceful bravado, identifying with it too, was how Synge put on the new man.

People on Inishmaan and its sister islands were primitive, meaning close to the verities. Synge brought the first alarm clock to the islands. Before then, islanders calculated time by the position of the sun. He brought a camera, snapping pictures of his neighbors, but when they saw him do this they turned self-conscious, like Indians in Peru who think the camera means to capture their souls. He loved the people but differed from them, not superior exactly, living on another plane. Both the love and the difference show in his plays.

Yeats, posting his apostles to the four corners, sent Synge to Aran. The year before the Abbey Theatre was founded, he called him home from his fugitive life on the Continent. "I said, 'Give up Paris, you will never create anything by reading Racine, and Arthur Symons will always be a better critic of French literature. Go to the Aran Islands. Live there as if you were one of the people themselves; express a life that has never found expression.'" Synge did as instructed and it loosed his tongue, as if the Holy Ghost had paid him a visit. Living among the people, he listened to and remembered their outlandish turns of phrase. The stories they told him were quick with minute details—he says this in his Aran book—and the plays that come later celebrate a world that is personal, palpable, and specific. In the Preface to the *Playboy*, he confesses his debt: "I am glad to acknowledge how much I owe to the folk-imagination of... the country people of Ireland." He expressed that folk imagination in a prose that comes close to poetry, and because his language is primarily a poet's, I put him higher than any other playwright since Congreve.

But I don't want to invoke "prose poetry," a hybrid and sterile. There is nothing in Synge of Meredith or Pater. He didn't count syllables or listen for the beat of the sentence. But his prose is hardly stenographic. He himself tells the story of listening to the kitchen girls through a chink in the floor of his bedroom in Wicklow, and it has done him harm and sowed confusion. His art is meditated, also learned, and owes something to the scholar who had studied Irish at Dublin's Trinity College. Though rooted in reality, "the root of all poetry," it is of course highbrow. He stood on the shoulders of Irish peasants, and this vantage enabled him. But he saw farther than they did.

Here, from his experience on Aran, is the kind of data he pulped and made into art: a mother's keening for her lost son, and the debate whether the clothing taken from a body that had been floating off the coast of Donegal belonged to the missing islander from Inishmaan; the fashioning of a coffin for the drowned man from boards that had been saved to make a coffin for an aged mother; omens and portents: a mother's glimpse of her dead son, riding a horse behind the man who was about to be drowned; and this letter from a Gaelic-speaking friend:

> Johneen, Friend of My Heart. A million blessings to you. It's a while ago since I thought of a small letter to write, and every day was going until it went too far and the time I was about to write to you. It happened that my brother's wife, Shawneen, died. And she was visiting the last Sunday in December, and now isn't it a sad story to tell? But at the same time we have to be satisfied, because a person cannot live always.

Out of this material, Synge created *Riders to the Sea*, the finest tragedy in English since the Age of Shakespeare.

\* \* \*

Tragedy in English died soon after Shakespeare, then the Puritans, not wanting it to revive again, sowed the ground with salt. Later the king came back, but tragedy didn't return with him, and a deep divide separates Synge's time and Shakespeare's. Serious comedy still diverted theatergoers until the end of the century, hanging on for some decades longer than that. In the eighteenth century there are Goldsmith and Sheridan, Goldsmith better than Sheridan, more flesh on his bones, but neither is up to Farquhar, dead long before both. After them comes a Dark Age of rubbish.

Its generic spokesman, an archetypal couch potato, thinks that truth is easy, as we say now, "to access." We needn't climb a mountain like the one Donne commits us to, cragged, steep, and sudden. All of us have the seeds of judgment within, and need only open our shirtfronts. Older generations looked for truth in the outside world, dense with particulars. But particulars being indigenous and each a law to itself, the new ideology gives them short shrift. Putting the general truth first, it does this in Latin, befitting the old days. "*Universalia ante rem.*"

Synge's plays, like Shakespeare's, turn that around, putting the particular in front of the general. They have a watchword too, "*Universalia post rem.*" Both proceed by analogy, likening one thing to another. Both are spendthrift of words, Shakespeare using a pair of them—"whiff and wind," "hire and salary," "single and peculiar"—when denotation needs only one. A famous critic of his in the next age said his whole style was "pestered with figurative expressions." But Dryden isn't sparing of figures himself. Only they don't clarify, functioning largely as icing on the cake.

Style is a way of thinking, not the "dress" of thought, and a style that doesn't point the moral but only adorns the tale isn't good for the health of the play. Fictitious problems absorb it, involving characters who aren't real but live in settings as real as the carpenter can make them. Trouble is in the offing when the curtain goes up and the audience claps for the stage set. "Virtual reality" is a phrase for this kind of theater.

The matrix Synge came from sponsored this spurious reality, at the same time producing men like him who called it into question. An image from Hamlet says how one lives inside the other, like a snuff within the candle's flame "abating" its strength. I think we are aware that a world more than merely verisimilar—doorknobs turning and teacups rattling in their saucers—is beginning to revive when Cardinal Newman puts a famous phrase front and center, "Felix qui potuit rerum cognoscere causas": "Happy the man who could understand the causes of things." In bringing up Newman, whose name isn't on everyone's lips, I feel like old Symmachus defending the pagan gods against the new dispensation. But *The Idea of a University* is worth making time for. Thick with matter of society, it creates a climate for plays.

Even "fuligenous" Carlyle (much smoke, not much fire) acknowledges a world that was there before he was. With him you have to qualify, though, and escaping Descartes, he runs us on Calvin. Carlyle doesn't have enough "cognoscere causas." Marx, another equivocal forerunner, has too much "rerum." But he knows that "Being determines consciousness, not consciousness being." The contrary saying, less a truth than a quibble, is Bishop Berkeley's, a hundred and some years before. "Esse est percipi," Berkeley tells us, giving the drama its quietus. "To be, is to be perceived."

In Shakespeare's world of theater, being antedates perceiving. It isn't a world of kings—that part, only history, is best left to historians—but a compacted mass made of earth, air, fire, and water. After a lapse of centuries we meet it again in Wilde, Shaw, and Synge.

One smacks less of earth than another, but each acknowledges a social fabric that is more than a painted cloth backing the stage. Each rubs against the world he lives in, amusing us or eliciting tears. In allowing Synge priority, I don't mean to diminish the others. But at its highest pitch his art is a more "spacious mirror" than theirs, reflecting both the bright side and its moiety of shadow.

\* \* \*

But what does it mean that Synge chose "the living world for text"? First of all it means that his plays are impure, like the categories Polonius tells of: "pastoral-comical, historical-pastoral, tragical-historical," and so on. The source of the *Playboy*, a true story (Connaught man kills his father with a spade), has all the realism of the police blotter. Synge turns this to comedy as he mines the "great gap between a gallous story and a dirty deed." His play is satire as the players, like the mob in Dublin, can't tell which is which. But it is tragedy as the heroine spells out the difference, too late.

The old *multiplex intelligentia*, most acute in Shakespeare, stages a comeback in Synge, and entertaining contrary truths, he holds them in suspension. It isn't tenable to speak of the gist of his plays. *In the Shadow of the Glen* reduces in paraphrase to a ribald folk tale, but gratuities add another dimension. Nora, who hears the herons crying over the black lakes, is more than an unfaithful wife. The heroine of the Playboy, itching and scratching, with a stink of poteen on her, is also a prize for the Lord God sitting lonesome in Heaven. Wistful, lyrical, and tender, she descends to savagery that makes us move back in our chairs. Who in the literature runs the gamut as she does? Cleopatra maybe.

Synge is too shrewd a playwright to bore us with criminals, but all in his play are capable of criminal behavior. He says this of the people of Aran, types of mankind. Only a poor good-for-nothing man would never hurt a fly, not true of the hero. His name stands for Christ, though, and the scene near the end where they drop the noose on his head affects us like the Jews' rejection of the Messiah. Christ is also Anti-Christ, and it's by the like of him that "the sins of the whole world are committed." The word we expect to hear is "forgiven."

Colleagues of Synge's squirmed at what he was showing them, and you can see why. In a political age he is a-political and believes in original sin. (I don't speak of the man but the plays.) Compassion is the other side of his unblinkered view, and giving no one just deserts, he vindicates our carnal humanity. His plays are prodigious, neither fish nor flesh but both together. In the comedies sadness is always an undersong, and in the tragedies the emotional direction is upward. Age will find his blurring of kinds more credible than youth.

*Deirdre of the Sorrows*, officially a tragedy, bears out its title. I think it does this too insistently, reminding us that Synge died before he could give it his final imprimatur. But I want to distinguish the play's special quality. Though the heroine dies and the lustful king will follow, an aureole of light surrounds its dark center. We hear "there are nights when a king like Conchubor would spit upon his arm ring, and queens will stick their tongues out at the rising moon." Not evading the ruin that comes to all in the end, *Deirdre of the Sorrows* directs attention to the "little corner" allowed us, between the daytime and the long night. *Antony and Cleopatra*, though far greater, is like this.

Synge's art is parochial, not a term of diminishment, and though he wasn't a nationalist he owes much to the patriotic impulse you find in the nationalist movement, Young Ireland. Jingoism isn't part of this, but love of the folk and the land. He studied Irish antiquities, and his learning has a cognate in the Gaelic scholarship of Sir Samuel Ferguson and Standish James O'Grady. Neither is remembered except by specialists but I name them because they tell us that Synge was a man of his time. He didn't look backward like some at the time, however, and the past led him on to the present. This meant writing plays for the new National Theater. Friends of his created it, and together they turned the world upside down.

Yeats wrote their memorial: "We three alone in modern times, John Synge, I, and Augusta Gregory." They thought all they did or sang "Must come from contact with the soil." It had to be Irish soil, however. "Soon after I had relinquished the kingdom of God I began," said Synge, "to take a real interest in the kingdom of Ireland." After that, "everything Irish became sacred."

But something is missing to explain the transformation of a failed aesthete to a great dramatist. Mere antiquarianism never created a good play or poem. The Irish revivalists, James Clarence Mangan, Douglas Hyde, and the early Yeats, deserve praise mostly for their pious intention. Look at Yeats's pseudo-Celtic verse, the painted poetry he started out with, and then recall the careful nature of Eliot's remark that Yeats became universal as he became more Irish. This doesn't mean more Irish in subject. It is the growth of a new expression in Yeats that matters. And new expression is the key to the flaring up of genius in Synge.

His triumph is essentially one of language, true of Shakespeare, though modern critical fashion denies this. Buck Mulligan in Joyce knows about Shakespeare, "The chap that writes like Synge." Each has his celebrated coups de theatre, as when Dan Burke, like Falstaff, rises from the dead, but a just estimate will say that for both of them, language is gesture. Neither chases after ideas. Father Reilly, the Holy Father, and the cardinals of Rome, none of whom we meet, are the villains of the Playboy, and a coat with nothing to fill it is the coat of a Christian man. Mostly, however, Synge is above polemic. You hear his true self in the laconic ending of *Riders to the Sea*: "No man at all can be living for ever, and we must be satisfied."

Get past the high coloring and you see how his plays are like old-fashioned opera, Gluck's, for instance, all aria and not much happening besides. The time he spent on French writers is generally dismissed as labor lost, but he got something from it, and his art resembles the neo-classical art of Racine. (Maybe this is what Cyril Cusack intends by imagining Synge the Parisian.) "Of all poets," said Valéry, "it is Racine who bears the most direct relationship to music proper—Racine, whose periods so often suggest recitative... Racine whose tragedies Lully went so studiously to hear, and of whose finest movements the beautiful forms and the pure developments of Gluck seem to be the immediate translations."

Music isn't translatable, and I have never read a translation of Racine that makes sense. I don't believe Synge would work in any language other than the one he created. But though he gives first place to words, his aren't merely pictorial nor are the plays felt as static. Whatever the dearth of action, his language is kinetic, its emphasis on the how, when, and where.

*The Well of the Saints*, taking off from the tale of a holy well that cured blindness, moves beyond anecdotage as it engages the senses. Really to live in them, Synge is telling us, we have to be blind. The saint who disputes this, not knowing the harm he does, is like those truth-tellers in Ibsen. But Synge is more than a realist, and the blindness he dramatizes, though literal, is a metaphor too. His Martin and Mary Doul, old blind beggars, are reconciled to it when they hear the yellow birds (whose song must sound yellow), feel the sun, and smell furze on the hill. In language that never insists but shakes us like trumpets, Synge is announcing the return of the physical world.

The *Playboy* is a metamorphosis story, and its climax comes when the hero puts off the old man. Sharing the stage with a false hero, he vivifies Shakespeare's phrase, "Minding true things by what their mockeries be." Like and unlike Christy, the Widow Quin kills her father when her rusty pick poisons his blood. Only a "dirty deed," this one shows the hero as he might be, before the action makes him over. Some, calling his transforming into question, locate it in the mind's eye. Right You Are If You Think You Are! But style is the man, no arguing with it. "Saying words would raise the topknot on a poet," Christy transforms himself. In some such way, the Word becomes Flesh.

\*    \*    \*

The shift in interest from the indefinite article to the definite, from *universalia ante rem* to the thing itself, lies behind the flowering of drama in English. Some exceptions there are, chiefly the Morality of the late Middle Ages—*Everyman* is the famous one—and the Expressionist plays of the earlier twentieth century, remembered in English for a few bad plays of O'Neill's. But mainstream drama, at least in our language, pays attention to the lower case, looking away from capital letters. This attention that must be paid is magical in its effect, and marks the development of the trope, late in the ninth century, into something like a legitimate play. A thousand years later, it marks Synge's transition from a rootless and featureless "European," a cipher, a nothing, to a particular Irish playwright.

The thing that asks recognition has to be seen close up: "a foolish hanging of the nether lip," hair "the like of a handful of thin grass... rotting where the wet lies, at the north of a sty." In *Riders to the Sea*, the problem is to give a name to the dead man pulled from the water. The flannel his clothes are made of isn't a help: "aren't there great rolls of it in the shops of Galway?" But the sister who is Synge's surrogate—she has a myopic eye—sees how his stockings are one of a kind. Putting up stitches, she counted three but dropped four, and this stocking is Michael's, the second of the third pair she knitted.

Bringing language down to homeliness lets Synge climb up high when he wants to. At the end of *Deirdre*, for example. Naisi the hero is dead, leaving "the whole world scorched," and why should Deirdre stay on "when no light in the heavens, and no flower in the earth under them, but is saying to me that it is Naisi who is gone forever." Comparing Shakespeare doesn't seem out of the way, e.g. Cleopatra's question, after the death of Antony: "Shall I abide/ In this dull world, which in thy absence is/ No better than a sty?" Readers who want their poetry high flown will hear this as a breach of decorum.

Much of Synge's writing, vulgar in St. Jerome's sense, is open to the charge. For the scene to be real, he has to stab it with his finger: there, "on the scruff of the hill." Gaining credibility from matter-of-fact, he sets his scene in motion. His characters aren't rained on but "out in the rain falling." Women don't grow old until we see "their white and long arms going from them." Christy Mahon in his best play has a quality name, "the like of what you'd find on the great powers and potentates of France and Spain." It's the participle and the adverb that work the magic for Synge.

# 3

# Painting by Numbers in Paul Valéry

Among twentieth-century poets, Valéry is the true son of Oscar. Don't speak to him of content, only a means to the end. This end is the creating of an autonomous artifact that transcends moral judgment and disavows paternity, as if poetry were born out of air. "Still worse and worse," as they say of mad Prince Hamlet, the poem possesses only such reality as is contained in "the play of figures." Circumscribed by conventions, "the mainspring of all games," it has a very limited purview ("Contemporary Poetry"). Valéry on poetry doesn't make the heart beat faster, and you can see why Eliot, the same who said that *Hamlet* was less Shakespeare's masterpiece than an artistic failure, esteemed him.

Few critics knew better how to needle the bourgeoisie. It isn't that, like Yvor Winters, he switches pantheons on us, but that he yanks the rug from under our most cherished prepossessions. Reverential readers of poetry got him going. "*Mais je m'en fous, moi, de la poesie,*" he said. "I don't give a damn for poetry." Many readers assume he was kidding. They think poetry improves us, and that a great poem demands a great thought. I used to quote with approval somebody who said this. But Valéry's ideal poem lives in a vacuum, aloof from history and at a temperature of absolute zero. "Pure poetry!" he called it, in a *cahier* (notebook entry) of the 1920s. "I started the expression going." This *fabrication*, another term he favored, had nothing to do with his life and was "absolutely devoid of ideas." He is commenting on his volume of 1922, *Charmes*, that is, "carmina" or songs or the charm of a beautiful woman. Among the poems in this volume, one craves attention, "Le Cimetière marin" ("The Graveyard by the Sea"), and he is letting us know how to take it.

His chilly comments notwithstanding, I have cared about the poem for a long time. In the matter of liking poetry, one doesn't have to give reasons; still, I find myself wondering why. Perhaps this is a case in which we should trust the tale, not the teller. Perhaps he is that hero manqué of contemporary criticism, the unselfconscious writer who wrote better than he knew or was willing to own up to. This "conflicted" poet at war with himself will appeal to sophisticated moderns. But before I deconstruct him, a look at his poem seems in order.

Though it educates its hero, let us agree not to call it a Bildungsroman. Valéry's poet-hero isn't born again, and the change that overtakes him isn't that absolute change we are witness to in born-again Christians. What he knows in the end he glimpses in the beginning. Superbly poised in the beginning—but his poise is like ice—he is of the party of the sea and sky, pure and aloof, hardly human. Irresistibly, however, the party of the dead compels his attention. Disgust wells in him as he entertains images of his own future corruption. On this negative note the poem might end. It does in "Adonais" or the "Elegy in a Country Churchyard," where the hero is dying or already dead. Tate's "Ode to the Confederate Dead," its eye on Valéry, ends with the serpent, a version of his "irrefutable" worm. But Valéry's ending is affectively happy.

Perhaps that is from wishing and willing, and he is tearing his pleasures through the iron gates of life, like Marvell in his "Coy Mistress." Violence is a way of getting out of the poem, for instance in Arnold's "Empedocles on Etna," where the hero at the end jumps into the volcano. But emotions need their counterpoise, the way every action needs its equal and opposite reaction, and Valéry's structure answers the need. "Joy after woe, and woe after gladness." No doubt he wished to be happy, though being lachrymose had its charms, but his beau ideal is structure and its requirement came first. Urgent with imperatives—*brisez, buvez, courons, envolez-vous, rompez* ("shatter," "drink," "run," "fly away," "break," twice repeated), his conclusion appeals to the present, ignoring what's to come.

A "monologue of self," he called the poem, making it easy to merge him with its hero. He said he wanted to show the effect on an adolescent boy of the sea and light of his native place, Sète, on the Mediterranean coast of France. This fishing port where he was born in 1871 is built against the sea on a narrow tongue of land, broken on its western edge by a steep hill. The graveyard of which he wrote and in which he was buried in 1945 lies on the hill's seaside slope. "This cemetery exists," he said, a few years after writing the poem. "It dominates the sea, on which one sees the doves, that is the fishermen's boats, wandering and pecking." To our surprise, however, none of this, except for the doves that are also fishing boats, gets into the poem. Criticism, said Wilde, is the only civilized form of autobiography, and Valéry is less writing his life than critiquing its materials.

He had different sides, and the poem seeks to keep them in balance. On one side he was Narcissus, the self-smitten man but filtered through a real young woman, dead before he was born. She was Narcissa, daughter of Edward Young, progenitor of the "Graveyard School of Poetry." Once everyone knew his "Night Thoughts," evoking "creation's melancholy vault,/ The vale funereal, sad cypress gloom." When his daughter died in Montpellier, he buried her in its Jardin des Plantes, where Valéry in his student days walked often. Contemplating her marble slab "brought on reveries in me," he said, the kind you would predicate of the self-conscious poet we meet in his "Graveyard by the Sea."

Already at sixteen he was writing: "I take delight endlessly in my own brain." It didn't stop delighting him, and later his narcissistic side found expression in Monsieur Teste. This hero of a philosophical tale he wrote in the 1890s is a head without a body. For years he labored to discover the laws of the mind, suspending life's normal round in the meantime. Valéry's life imitates this fiction, just as Wilde would have prescribed. Beginning in 1892 he quit on poetry, entering on the "Great Silence," a period of intense mental cultivation lasting twenty-five years. Soon after he came out of it, he wrote his famous poem. In the poem his shadow passes over the mansions of the dead, getting him used to the ghostly thing he saw himself turning into.

But the body brings in its revenges against the self-mortified man, and on his flesh-and-blood side, Valéry understood this. His problem was technical, the besetting one for him: how to keep his different sides, physical and cerebral, from destroying the poem's integrity. Addressing the problem led him to philosophy and the paradoxes of Zeno, the arrow which flies but is stationary at any moment, so never moves at all, and giant-striding Achilles, outrun by a tortoise's shadow. Intellectual conundrums, they blow into the poem like a gust of wind, an arid wind, no doubt, balancing the morbid talk of "graves, of worms, and epitaphs," and the fervid sexuality that follows. In the same way the sexuality oversets the philosophy, neither being autobiographical, or not first of all, but present for reasons of structure. Also it shatters, almost as parody might, the long and painful meditation on the gap between life's glamour, *l'art personnel*, and the loathsome thing it becomes. Valéry the régisseur has his hands on all these ropes, anyway he says so.

He had another side, both insouciant and humble, and I notice it here from affection. It doesn't energize the poem like the Hic and Ille of his opposing selves; it pervades the poem, however, and suggests why we read it. In the carnage of the First World War, when a friend wondered what he was doing now, he answered: "I am varnishing old poems.... it is the kind of work done by Latin versifiers, masticating hexameters during the times of Attila the Hun and Genseric the Vandal. For whom? For what?" A reason to like him is that he left the questions unanswered.

The principal motive he assigned to his masterpiece wouldn't occur to most readers. He said he wanted to fill a rhythmic figure with syllables that resisted being put into prose, and "noticed that this figure was decasyllabic." "Noticed" is nice. But never mind the negligent pose, his choice of a figure wasn't accidental. The strict decasyllabic form is "foreign to our souls," he wrote, "and as it were deaf to our desires." They want to emancipate our feelings, letting them all hang out. Against the feelings, however, form imposes its requirements. They were "half-mad," he said, and incite us to rebellion. But as the poem discovers, the requirements are good and the rebelling is good, both violence and the containing of it being critical for its success.

Unlike young Wordsworth in another monologue of self, Valéry didn't aim at recording the growth of a poet's mind. He wanted to make. Don't look for an object: the verb is intransitive, and it is the intention of making which wants what he says. This sounds like a tongue twister, but I am sticking close to his words and perhaps their sense is clear enough. The poet is a maker, like any other wright, boatwright, cartwright, playwright. His craft of making imposes technical obligations, and meeting them gets priority, while self-expression takes a back seat. This is cold but appropriate to art, and Valéry's bias is less benevolent than artistic.

* * *

But though his poem doesn't mirror the life, the life helps us see into the poem. He liked being tethered, with the tether cut shorter than need be. Much of his work is *ouvrage de commande*, tailored to suit a commission. He was an opportunist like many great ones, Dr. Johnson, for instance, who boasted that he could write the life of a broomstick. Partly, I suspect, commissioned work agreed with Valéry's strengths and weaknesses, strong on the executive side, relatively weak in his imaginative faculty. No poet's eye in a fine frenzy rolling.

Skimping on action, his poem resembles old-fashioned opera, one of Gluck's, a favorite composer. I see it as like Gluck's version of Orpheus and Eurydice, he walking up an incline away from the underworld, she trailing along behind him. Every so often, they stop to sing. Though things happen—the poet climbs up to a high place, exposes his soul to the torches of noon, looks over the grave-yard—the language that reports them is less visual than auditory, e.g. the hissing of sibilants when brilliant Heaven sows its disdain on the sky ("La scintillation sereine sème/ Sur l'altitude un dédain souverain, stanza 4"). Racine and Seneca among poets are like this, the former ranking high on his list.

Music was the great art, Valéry thought, but architecture in its purest state seemed more nearly complete because it had nothing left over. Architecture means blueprints, the ghostly paradigm rather than its manifestations, and though he gave it first place, it wasn't his metier. He isn't good on the Pisgah-sight or getting up into the watchtower; he likes to peep and botanize, lowering his eyes. Struc-ture looms large, but as a goal, not a faculty. "Le Cimetière marin" seems to validate this judgment, the first twenty-one of its twenty-four stanzas going downward, only the last three ascending. Dia-lectical poems like "Sunday Morning" canvass points of view, in this way reaching their resolution, but Valéry's performs a volte face.

His universe of poetry is peopled by images, linked turns of speech and rhythms, consonance, dissonance. (I am drawing on his account of it in his essay on the poem.) Ideas play their part but as supernumeraries, "by no means the chief object of... (a poem's) discourse." Pure prose, on the other hand, is occupied exclusively with saying something. It doesn't want to make or be a medium, it wants to convey a message. Once the message is transmitted, the words that convey it have no reason to linger. The end of pure prose "is the tendency toward a uniform mental substitution" ("Commentaries on *Charmes*"). That is, it works its own extinction, and that is all there is to say about meaning.

But the form has a charm of its own, and Valéry shifts the emphasis towards it. The reality of his writing is confined to words and forms, though, as he tells us, "What is 'form' for anyone else is 'content' for me." It pleases readers to suppose that he put intellectual coin in their purse, but he didn't offer to teach them, and Boileau's claim that his poetry always said something opened for him on "an infinity of horrors." You have to watch him, however, a sly Valéry who liked blowing up his reader. The poet who despised teaching wrote of poetry in his notebooks that "it is nourishing," though its "thought must be hidden in verse like the nutritive essence in fruit." This sounds like the long-held heresy, still around today, that sees poetry as a sugarcoated bolus. But Valéry only appears to entertain it. "Enchantment," he continues, without batting an eye, "that is the nourishment poetry conveys."

His frivolity, though partly teasing, verges on heartlessness, and his criticism seems written by a man handling sugar tongs. In his discussion of "Le Cimetière marin," though he says he derives the poem's language from life, we feel that that is faute de mieux. Putting life in its place, he defines it as "this statistical disorder." Did he lack something of our everyday humanity? I think so. His reiterated interest in Racine's *Phèdre* isn't nearly as impassioned as his lack of interest in Racine's love affairs. Outside Sète fishermen farm the famous Bouzigues oysters, and in restaurants along the canal the bouillabaisse is fantastic. But Valéry, New Critical to the nth power, leaves all that to one side.

A lot of what matters drops out in his poetics. Eliot, though an admirer, detected in him the macaroni or elegant trifler, who "provides us with no criterion of seriousness." Problems of process concerned him deeply, but he isn't much concerned with the poem's relation to life. Rational to a fault was the judgment of Wallace

Stevens, a pot calling the kettle black. His Valéry is through-and-through Apollonian, and Dionysus doesn't comport with his genius. But toward the end of the great poem, Dionysus shoulders his way into it, smashing the lofty conceits of the intellect to powder. The wave, driven by the rising wind, presents the unruly god, and the poet enlists in his service. One of the high priests in the religion of art, he finds his long-held faith too constricting, and his psychology too impoverished, innocent of the imperatives that keep body and soul together. Renouncing the neoclassical *règles* of Racine— and, let us add, of his eighteenth-century forebear, English Edward Young—he opts for the shapelessness associated with life. Meanwhile his Apollonian side is parked outside the gate, motor idling.

* * *

In this unheroic way he made contact with the springs of our being. James Merrill has him enduring fruitless days, empty-seeming like his deracinated self. But the roots of his days run deep— Merrill's poem says they delve deep in the waste, that is, the Graveyard by the Sea, the real one and the one he wrote of. You find them at the world's heart, "Still tracking that profound/ Water the heights require" ("Paul Valéry: *Palme*"). I grant it sounds pietistic, this picture of the poet ascending from the depths to the heights. But the earth he ascends from stays with him, both his limitation and the condition of his success.

Wallace Stevens is like that, and I find it almost inevitable to read the two poets together. Edgar Bowers, a modern poet worth keeping, introduced me to Valéry and Stevens half a lifetime ago. I could wish the hammers were still beating in his lively brain. But like that univocal Winters whose student he was, he took a dim view of qualifying judgments, and perhaps his "*Gott in Himmel!*" would have greeted my version of Stevens. It says that most of his poetry goes in one direction, the best of it going in another. He rephrased the same philosophical music until death stopped his voice, and who will doubt its distinction. But he chased a fatal chimera for which he lost the world and was willing to lose it. This was the impulse to abstraction.

I must qualify, however, and the great poems of Harmonium, in particular *Sunday Morning* and *Le Monocle de Mon Oncle*, put a different Stevens before us. They seem to me sui generis in the context of his oeuvre, though he thought of it, paradoxically, as "the whole of Harmonium," a fulfilling and completing of the volume he published first. It isn't easy to read these poems without involving the body—getting up from the chair, staring out the window "with a wild surmise." The blank verse, unequalled in English since Tennyson's "Ulysses," evokes a physical world and the feeling that entertains it, investing the poems like a nimbus. Quoting from *Le Monocle de Mon Oncle*:

> Like a dull scholar, I behold, in love,
> An ancient aspect touching a new mind.
> It comes, it blooms, it bears its fruit and dies.
> This trivial trope reveals a way of truth.
> Our bloom is gone. We are the fruit thereof.
> Two golden gourds distended on our vines,
> We hang like warty squashes, streaked and rayed,
> Into the autumn weather, splashed with frost,
> Distorted by hale fatness, turned grotesque.
> The laughing sky will see the two of us
> Washed into rinds by rotting winter rains.

Perhaps no American poems of the twentieth century climb higher than these two, discursive but tilting toward Dionysus. Stevens, laboring his craft for many years after, never reached the same heights again.

Valéry's language, though I try to do it justice, must in part elude me: it isn't mine. But I think I see far enough into him to say that he won his greatest triumph in poetry as he put off the intellectualizing habit. Intellectualizers don't use but misuse the intellect, "trying decapitation from the body bush"—John Crowe Ransome's phrase in his Phi Beta Kappa poem at Harvard. The poem suggests Monsieur Teste, Valéry as he might have been. "Le Cimetière marin," leaving M. Teste behind, is Valéry 's least "selfish" poem (says Marcel Muller) as it turns from brooding on the mind to honor the claims of the body.

With all this, its maker is of the middle class that produced him, grudging with words, approving the vulgar tongue, deep down a patriot. Replying to Georges Duhamel, who found his writing not involved enough in the time of the First World War, he said he wrote to leave a monument to a language that might perish should

Germans win the war. People who thought his poetry abstruse didn't know how he cultivated ordinary speech, even argot, like the language of sailors. A boat plunging forward is seen as pecking like a bird: "ou picoraient des focs!" in the last stanza of "Le Cimetière marin," recalling the doves with which the first stanza begins. Swimming on a sea that looks like a rooftop, doves come into the poem via a child's tale of a bird that drowns when it mistakes a pool of water for a roof to perch on.

But the niggarding way with words isn't simply provincial and tells also of the stylist who meant everything to count. Still more qualification is in order, however, and he had a lavish spirit, proper to a poet who first came before his public in the Belle Epoque. An air of prodigality distinguishes his writing, in excess of what the facts of the case require. He is a wordsmith, and belongs in the company of Stevens and Montale. He does credit to this company, and the other way round. Sometimes, like the others, he works our confusion. But thrift is ruinous in the economy of the spirit, an apothegm of his, and the prodigals are the ones who grow rich.

Like Montale, he tasted ashes in his mouth ("je goûte à la cendre"), so enjoined on himself his own annihilation. "Take the shape of absence" is his counsel in his longest poem, *La Jeune Parque* ("The Youngest of the Fates"). But his psychology is affirmative, anyway more or less. Everyone remembers the thrilling close of "Le Cimetière marin," almost an imperative, not quite: "Il faut tenter de vivre." After all, it's necessary to live. *La Jeune Parque* seems to echo this: "il le faut, ô Soleil, Que j'adore mon coeur où tu te viens connaître": "It is necessary, O Sun, That I adore my heart wherein you are confirmed." Valéry is countervailing, in any case he is counterpointing, the injunction to descend and to sleep. The countervailing is partly rhetorical, and he is less an intellectual than an incantatory poet.

With his belittling of ideas goes a partiality for rhetoric—"the blackbird whistling" is Stevens's phrase. Putting the two together throws a light on the way he composed. His own account seems merely paradoxical, as when, quoting his master Mallarmé, he ushers content out the door, "no longer the cause of the 'Form' but one of the effects." *La Jeune Parque* "evolved," he said, "from the 'form' towards the 'content.'" The quotation marks setting off the key words are his and say that he read them with a difference. In "Le Cimetière

marin," the form "proposed, or almost imposed, a subject." This is
a radical statement of the case, and would seem to affront common
sense.

Prof. Rene Wellek, a scholar-critic whose opinion is sometimes
worth having, thought Valery's proposition more striking than true.
But Valéry's eye is on heaven, and you don't make it into the small
corner of heaven reserved for critics by qualifying your obiter dicta.
He knew this and his are swingeing. Like Oscar's, however, they
clarify truth while appearing to deride it. The negligent manner,
though offensive and meant to be, masks the high seriousness of
an artist who thought art too important to be left to professors.

Like every credentialed artist, he understood that art begins with
technique. Often what "the duncves" call a profound idea (the sneering word is his) "arises from the need to link up two stanzas, two
developments of a theme." Composition when it works is rife with
encounters between the arbitrary requirement—call it the form—
and the hard-pressed but dutiful artist. Like Lazarus come back
from the dead, he has something to tell us. But accepting his
craftsman's obligation: fitting his neck to the yoke of meter or rhyme,
he finds that he has hit on the "truth."

Readers with an ear for metrics will understand how the four-
foot line, for example, is appropriate to epigram, even demanding
it or something like it, whether elegant or risible. But it won't accommodate poetry which aims at discursive thought. So forms have
their decorum, and every poet must feel this. "Le Cimetière marin"
began with some such perception. It came to Valéry "in the shape"
of a composition in six-line stanzas, each line ten syllables long.
This shape he ended up with, and he distributed through it the content it needed to suggest a meditation by a particular self. Maybe or
maybe not the self was moi-même.

His form is like a cenotaph, already there and empty, awaiting a
"body" of thought. But not passively. It engenders its thoughtful
content, the way a man in the toils finds his courage. A saying of
Oscar Wilde's is dinning in his head: "Form, which is the birth of
passion, is the death of pain." In this two-part formulation, the second part is easy. Only order your misery and you free yourself
from it, says Aristotle, mediated by Freud. But what does it mean,
that form is the birth of passion? It takes a wright or craftsman to
say.

Seeing into Wilde (if he didn't know him in the letter, he knew him in the spirit), Valéry revises to read: "Beautiful works are daughters of their form, which is born before they are." His gnomic utterance needs a gloss, and he supplies it in a letter of the Twenties, describing another of his literary chores, *sur demande*. For a collection of engravings, he had agreed to furnish the text, limited to precisely 115, 800 letters. His first attempt ran over; he cut it, falling too short. The job went on like that, until he reached his quota.

Getting there was half the fun and he welcomed "these exigencies," not a penance but a release. They made him think of Greek sculptors at work on the Parthenon. Though "obliged to house their Olympian personages inside the obtuse triangle of pediments," they never complained. Accepting the obligation, they filled the space inside its bounding lines with figures. The figures, belonging on a pediment, took their character from it.

In this way or in a way analogous to it, Valéry's poem moved from line lengths and stanzas, the bare-bones image he saw in his mind's eye, to the composition that fell from his hands. In his essay on the poem, he tells how an importunate friend snatched it away, still unfinished. But the crucial part, a given, was there before he started to write. What he wanted to write was something else, possibly not to the purpose. Surprisingly, he wanted to write best-selling novels, but found them beneath or beyond him. Give him a plot, however, and he set to, filling in the details. The artistic process as he describes it sounds oddly like painting by numbers.

\* \* \*

Valéry was "the representative poet, the symbol of the poet, of the first half of the twentieth century," Eliot said. Though Yeats or Rilke might be greater, he stood for his time. He did this in his preoccupation with form, the characterizing feature of the modern age. "Le Cimetière marin," the poem of Valéry's readers will know if they know him at all, isn't natural but man made, like a frieze on a pediment. Mind is written all over it, and that is why we take it to heart.

An impersonal artist who says nothing in his own voice, Valéry is step by step deeply intentional. His intention isn't didactic but eleemosynary, however, as when Bach makes his music for the greater glory of God and the innocent pleasure of man. Registering point of view, recycled words and phrases are like leitmotifs in music, heard the second time round with a difference. As the poet returns the sun to its place in the heavens ("Je te rends," stz. 7), tone is dismissive, but it shifts dramatically when, at the climax, his soul is given back to him ("Me rend mon âme," 22). The sun, encountered for the first time, is the giver of light ("rendre la lumière," 7), and the focus of almost worshipful attention. But the girls we hear of later are far more compelling as they give their lips to their lovers ("se rendent," 16).

Point counterpoint, however, and lovers who trust to the lying hue of our flesh are deluded, embracing a dream. "Songe" and "mensonge," dream and falsehood, surface more than once, each repetition bringing with it an increment of meaning. As the poem unfolds, we see that these near homonyms are synonyms too, their relation verified in the undertaker's fictions ("beau mensonge," 18), all that crepe and gold hiding the empty skull. Valéry's poem is a tissue of words, not "the dress of thought" but the thought *tout entier*, and the poet must be alive to their whole lexical range. No point in asking him about his ulterior meaning: he doesn't have any. It's what's up front that counts.

A recurring word, *absents* (and its permutations) is thick with possible meanings, but they don't point all one way. Absent in the fruit ("il change son absence," 5) when the mouth chews and dissolves it, form is absent in life itself, drunk with the impulse to non-being ("ivre d'absence," 12). Subsequently the dead are absent, melted into a gross nothingness ("une absence épaisse," 15), and the gift of life that quickened them passes to the flowers. Often in poetry this is put for consolation, in Wilde's *Ballad of Reading Gaol*, for instance. But not in Valéry. His vision of life running away is touched with horror, and his "Où sont des morts": "Where are the dead?" (15) echoes Villon in the "Ballad of Dead Ladies." "But where are the snows of yesteryear?"

Valéry is even more poignant, though. The phrase he uses is "des morts," "of the dead," not a collective, not "les morts," but telling of particular persons whose special characteristics are focussed on, setting them apart. Emphasis goes to a familiar turn of speech or personal grace, a soul distinct from everyone else's. The absence of this is painful but not exclusively, and just here the poem declares its comprehensiveness, like the mingled yarn of our life. For the pain of loss, though it isn't ameliorated, has another aspect, different from its opposite but part of the whole. In some such way, the disjoint halves of a Picasso portrait confront each other. Death is abhorrent, but pleasure seems contingent on the loss of form, a Dionysiac apprehension, perhaps on the side of entropy. You wouldn't predicate it of Apollonian Valéry, except that he is himself and other selves too. What his poem laments it celebrates, and heaven chants to the consumed soul the deliquescence of all things (5).

But the poem's meanings don't change: they dilate, becoming more ample. At first the sun's light is perfect, "pure" (2,7), but this all-purpose word is debased coinage linguistically, and on a second look the sun's unfiltered light counts against it. Its lack of nuance or "chiaroscuro" distorts, and a great line conveys this: "Mais rendre la lumière/ Suppose d'ombre une morne moitié. "But to give light supposes a dark moiety of shade." Unalloyed in its purity, the light-giver of the opening lines is insufficiently itself, lacking a dark underside. Valéry might put it that the major key needs the minor to make a total composition. His poem is like that, impure or "nicely mixed" (Shakespeare's phrase for the whole man), and opposites share the honors between them. After the expansive heaven, "Beau ciel, vrai ciel" (6), focus narrows to a clamor in a vault, "amère, sombre, et sonore" (8).

Often, as here, sound echoes sense: all those open vowels that bring the meaning home to the ear. But the relation is like that of two horses running tandem, and sometimes it seems as if sound is the lead horse. For a rhetorical poet who belittles content and is anti-discursive, that mightn't surprise us. As his poem begins, sun and sea cast their spell, signalized by words that flow into each other like music: "recommencée, recompense," the last telling of the poet's reward for hard thinking. Initially his thought ("une pensée") is disembodied, suiting a connoisseur of abstractions. Later, however, he thinks of his ancestors ("pense à mes absents," 9), palpably there in the bony soil of the graveyard.

Bodies in the graveyard can't hold their shape, and words, partaking of one another, seem mimetic of this burning cauldron: "tant...tant/ plaît, dominé/ lumière... lieu" (10). In other passages Valéry's language is jingling and riddle-like: "temple simple,"/"tuiles, Toit" (3), undercutting his denotative meaning. Inspecting the sky at noon, he sees a "complete head," but the clacking sound his French makes, "Tête complète" (13), belies this. Jostling each other, "gardes" and "regard" (1,3,4) tell of perception, though the context calls it in question. In the description of Zeno, the philosopher of changelessness, words make a sounding emblem whose burden isn't stasis but change. "Pages of illustrations," says Wallace Stevens cavalierly, and let me leave it to the reader to check.

Like the Hydra of the penultimate stanza, the poem bites its tail, completing a circle. At first a stultifying *pensée* holds the poet captive but at last he rejects it, breaking the pensive mold ("cette forme pensive," 22). Confronting the heat and torpor of the beginning, the sea's fresh exhalation blows it away at the end. In this happy ending a book is before us, its sun-dazzled pages ("tout éblouies," 24) advertising the poet's choice of life over death. We remember how it was with him, oppressed by dazzling secrets ("secrets éblouissants," 9) that intimated his mortality. The opening words of the poem's first line, "Ce toit tranquille," are repeated in its last line, making us bear witness to the distance we've come. As life advances its claim, the quiet roof where the fishing boats forage is shattered.

But if this sounds too pat, it is, and the poem is more complicated than paraphrase suggests. Linguistically, the sequence is from negative to positive, and the ending repudiates the beginning. It does this only partly, however. The powerful imagery that signals the ending is bifold in its allegiance, on the side of life but also of death. This is where its power comes from, like that of the savage who eats his enemy's heart.

Case in point, the Hydra (23). Making us think of the phoenix that never dies, it is drunken and feeds on itself, so makes us think of the flesh-eating worm (20). Inebriated by life, it resumes the evacuated world of the graveyard (12), where life is drunk with the idea of non-being. As these resemblances multiply, it becomes apparent that the brightening world of the ending doesn't oppose but complements the moribund world we begin with. Folding back on itself, the poem shows these opposites-by-convention joining hands.

Stevens in a noble passage from "Sunday Morning" speaks to Valéry, one great spirit saluting another across cultures. Sometimes this happens across centuries, bridging a great gap in time. But here is the passage from Stevens, and though it hardly gives the gist of Valéry, no such thing, it suggests how these two make a pair: "Death is the mother of beauty, mystical,/ Within whose burning bosom we devise/ Our earthly mothers waiting, sleeplessly." Womb and tomb make a nexus (the rhyme is Shakespeare's in *Romeo and Juliet*), life flowing into death, death into life. In terms of Valéry's poem: Zeno's feathered arrow, piercing the poet like the eating worm, bestows life and reclaims it, its humming sound giving birth ("Le son m'enfante," 21) but killing as the arrow goes nowhere.

Valéry calls this philosopher "cruel," proposing that his paradox annuls the chance for life. But against Zeno is Heraclitus, the philosopher of change, who isn't physically there in the poem but is nonetheless decisive for its point of view. Helping to determine what this is, the poem on its lexical side cashes for us, its ambiguous punctuation, its phrases that look backwards and forwards, the way words deny their integrity even as the poet asserts it. "All things are a-flowing, sage Heraclitus says," remembering Pound in *Mauberly*, another modern classic worthy to stand with Valéry's.

I wouldn't describe his point of view as sanguine, but it sees a chance for life in the unending back and forth of negative and positive, "Non" and "Oui" (22, 23). Running forward, we are hurled back in a tumult like silence, then we reenter the game, "rentre dans le jeu!" (16) Two cheers for the game. "Il faut tenter de vivre!" says the poet, in the poem's most reverberant line. "Let us live, at any rate try to" (24).

The imperial sun, stationary at noon in the poem's early stanzas and inimical to life, is taken down a notch as the poem widens out. Its widening is like a river's running for the sea, and astonishment coincides with the ending. Though hobbled by carnality and creeping towards dissolution, our painfully human soul gets the palm. It can hardly match the sun's majesty, fortified as it is with "the calm of the gods" (1), but other things muster in its support, the bird-sharp cries of girls, divine impatience that dies as it quickens, one man's penitence, his doubts, and compulsions, "Mes repentirs, mes doutes, mes contraintes" (14). All this is the stuff of life, and though it won't last, asks attention.

After Valéry died, a well-meaning functionary caused a pair of verses from the first stanza of "Le Cimetière marin" to be inscribed on his tomb. "O récompense après une pensée/ Qu'un long regard sur le calme des dieux!" reads the inscription, its punctuation typically vexed. "O recompense after a thought/ Is a long glance at the calm of the gods!" Though the functionary didn't know this, "the calm of the gods" is death, an irony Valéry would have relished.

# 4

# The Poetry of Eugenio Montale

Montale is Italy's greatest modern poet, and belongs with the generation that came to public notice just before and after the First World War. Like Wallace Stevens a *parolaio* or dandy in language, he fetches words from the Latin inkhorn, at the other end of the spectrum from popular argot. Like Eliot, he looks on the dark side, and boredom and horror are always in the offing. Sometimes they join forces. In a poem from his third book, *La Bufera e Altro*, the President of the Immortals throws down his mask and the box of surprises is opened. The melodrama is like Thomas Hardy, a persistent resemblance. Montale's sinister-offhanded title participates in it: "The Storm Etc."

Not a prolific writer, he "blotted" as much as he wrote—five volumes of poems published incrementally over fifty years, each engorging thriftily smaller collections appearing since the last major statement; a volume of anecdotal prose sketches; translations, conspicuously of poetry in English. A man of formidable silences, he wasn't called a Hermetic poet for nothing. "There should be an eleventh commandment," he said: "don't bother people." He himself owed allegiance to this commandment, unlike the self-promoters who are the bane and definition of the artistic life in our time.

Born in 1896, he served in the First World War as an infantry officer. He began to publish in the twenties, "anni mirabiles." The Fascists forced him out of his librarian's job in Florence, and he turned to translating poetry in English. Some of his poets are Emily Dickinson, Hardy, Hopkins, Eliot, and Shakespeare. When you get to know him, you see how they cash. After the Second World War he moved to Milan, where he worked as literary and music critic for Italy's best newspaper, *Corrière della Sera*. In 1976 he won the Nobel Prize for Literature. He died in 1981. Like our best poet in English, he is a monument without a tomb, and we can ignore as irrelevant the formal entry in the necrology pages.

Read him for long and you are likely to find yourself asking: "Chi me lo fa fare?" "Who got me into this?" His poetry is vatic, often hard to construe, and you understand a fury in his words but not the words. Old Greek poets, called "vates," are like him, their poet's eye in a fine frenzy rolling. "All you get here is some twisted syllable," he says in his first volume, *Cuttlefish Bones* (1925). The twistedness is like a tree limb's, "come un ramo," knotted all the way through.

A native of Genoa and the storm-swept Ligurian coast, he is the equivalent in Italian ethnology, vulgar style, of a tightfisted Scot. Like Hugh MacDiarmid, the voice of Scottish Gaeldom, he squeezes such value as he can from stunted flowers that grow in the wasteland. Italians like to tell about the starving Genovese, holed up in a mountain cabin in the dead of winter. He is resigning himself to the end when he hears a knock on the door. "Qui é?" It is the Red Cross to the rescue. But the arrival of help puts the penurious man on his guard. You don't get something for nothing. The Genovese says: "Ho gia da." "I've already given."

Readers who stick with Montale won't be sorry, however. Some poems of his will still be giving pleasure "Dum Capitolium scandet," "While the High Priest climbs the Capitol," as Horace used to tell us in school. Among the early ones are "The Sunflower" ("Portami girasole"), and "The Lemons," on the short list of the century's permanent poems. Both are typical Montale in allowing but truncating the ecstatic moment. In the first poem, Clizia the heliotrope, yearning toward Apollo, merges in his godhead. This is "the chance of all chances," life burning or vaporizing into its essence. The echo is of Pater, concluding *The Renaissance* ("To burn always with this hard, gemlike flame, to maintain this ecstasy, is success in life"), and Montale, though saturnine, is very Pateresque.

In "The Lemons" the chance of chances waits on a round of forgettable hours, rain and winter tedium, a miserly sun. "Quando un giorno":

When one day through a half-closed gate
among the greening branches of a courtyard
the yellows of the lemons open themselves;
and the ice of the heart vanishes,
and their songs,
golden trumpets of solarity,
burst like rolling thunder in the breast.

This is the leaven of Montale's poetry. If you will allow the hom-onym, it is the levin or lightning that irradiates but only for a single pulse of the artery the emptiness from which we come and which waits to reclaim us, "when it is time."

Robert Bly has a lucky title for Montale's second book of po-ems, *Le Occasioni* (1939). "The Instances," Bly calls it, iridescent moments when the divine enters in. Montale's instances are exem-plary, as when I "instance" this or that, also few and abridged. Seated at a remote table, he writes "from the honey cell of a sphere launched into space." ("News from Amiata") The sphere is the world, buf-feted by storms. "Outside it is raining." Later, in an interview, Montale saw the world as "like a projectile launched in an air without force of gravity," so flying through a dead sky forever. Ask him to tell you who set this flight in motion and he answers, "Che ne so io?" "How would I know?" Still, he makes room for the honey.

If I had to choose one poem from the poetry of the later years, I would choose "The Eel," absolute Montale in its arid and desolate landscape, quickened by "Love's arrow on earth." Like that re-spectful Mozart who doesn't come facilely to his highest points and doesn't stay with them, Montale is always sliding off. "Finchè un giorno": "Until one day"! In this operatic phrase, more persua-sive for being ventured so seldom, the poem prepares its shining climax. Making for "our estuaries" from the frozen Baltic, the eel moves always against the current, under the hostile flood, negotiat-ing parched gullies only moistened with slime, threading its way into the heart of the flint. Then abruptly, as light darted from the blossoming chestnuts burns in the stagnant ponds, the dead revive and the progress of this green spirit announces our own. It says that "everything begins when everything seems turned to carbon."

But putting it like that nails down a too-hopeful sense. Provi-sional is a word for Montale. In "The Hitler Spring," candles blanch the horizon, disfigured by horror, and maybe augur a new dawn. A bud stripes the air, auguring the descent of the angels of Tobias. Their office is to open our eyes but they don't get thanked for this, since what we see is refracted through lenses of tears. There isn't any help for the tears, and at any rate they cleanse perception. In a poem of Cavafy's, a mother prays to Our Lady for the safe return of the sailor who has already drowned. Meanwhile "the ikon listens, solemn, sad,/ knowing the son she waits for never will come back." This gives us the gritty gist of Montale, except that in his poetry the ikon is only an ikon.

He is remarkably constant to his tentative vision, and in the long career nothing changes much. Only the manner grows more patient, not of answers but questions. I imagine the acolyte who always sits at the feet of the great man, putting these questions. E.g., "What is Life?" "The Hawks," a permanent poem of the late 1960s, raises the question but only in metaphor, denying the chance for definitive statement. Life, incarnate in a scuffle of soft plumes, tears itself to pieces, so breaks momentarily from the unendurable web that confines it. The king of fishers, glimpsed in *Il Diario* (1973), signals this moment.

> I have seen more than one of them
> bring to the slime of the pools
> flashes of lapis lazuli.

The kingdom from which the bird or deity streaks like an arrow, invincible and evanescent—the qualifier "imprendibile" allowing either reading or both—is measured in millimeters. Montale thinks the measure is just.

His parsimony sets him against his century's reckless impulse to squander. Through-and-through skeptical, he believes that reality consists in what he sees. (He describes himself in one of the *Xenia* poems, a part of *Satura*, 1971, commemorating the death of his wife.) His autobiographical reflections are called *Racconto d'uno sconosciuto*—The Narrative of a Stranger. "Persistence is only extinction," says his "Little Testament," "little" putting it mildly. His first gesture, when he got the Nobel Prize, was to disconnect the telephone.

But though he doesn't believe much, he believes intensely, in the sense of a man bearing witness. What he witnesses to is the revitalizing power of the past, rising in judgment against the present. Compelling us to remember that "something happened . . . which is everything," he shakes the living dead in their shrouds. Like Yeats, who wanted to do this, he is a gravedigger, thrusting his buried ancestors back into the human mind. Madame Mandelstam in her memoirs glosses his central preoccupation as a poet: "A country in which people have been engaged in mutual destruction for half a century does not like to recall the past. What can we expect to happen in a country with a disordered memory? What is a man worth if he has lost his memory?" Montale is luckier than Osip Mandelstam, so able to address himself to these questions. No doubt the past is enveloped in shadows, maybe a nullity. Still he thinks it possible "to love a shadow, as we ourselves are shadows."

*     *     *

I read Montale for the first time in the New Directions paperback, English on one side, Italian on the other. He was already an international presence, and when he turned eighty the kingdom of letters took note. By then I had a *borsa* at the Villa Serbellone in Bellagio, overlooking Lake Como. Not far away in Milan, Montale was plying his poet's trade, in the severely classical setting created by Bramante around the Duomo. I wanted to see him plain, like young Robert Browning, thinking of Shelley. "And did he stop and speak to you?/ And did you speak to him again?"

More than once I nerved myself to knock on Montale's door and brave his notorious housekeeper Gina. A real Cerberus, people said she was. But I feared to intrude, to my credit perhaps, and a little while later he died. It would have been gratifying to shake my hero's hand, fodder for cocktail parties back home. Whether I'd have seen him plain is another matter.

For the way to know a poet isn't through the life but the work. Indifferent himself to celebrity status, Montale thought the artist's personality had little to do with his art. Meeting Brancusi, whose vociferous ego was everywhere in the room, he said, "This is precisely the problem of our time: art 'with anecdote' (that is, with something that recalls the life of the man)." Montale in real life was a soldier, a senator in Italy's Parliament (like Yeats in Ireland's), a would-be singer of bel canto. None of this says why we remember him. A version of the Creator, impassioned but impersonal, he hides in his handiwork, and you must look for him there. The impersonality authorizes the passion.

He has been dead now long enough to sift him, distinguishing his wheat from his chaff and he himself from his peers, past and present. He came on stage, like Yeats and Wordsworth, in a time outworn. His *dolce stil nuova* is a mixed style, meant to rejuvenate language and sensibility. Literary and homely words jostle one another, making for mutual refreshment, as in the little exercise in self-deprecation, "Il Pirla." Jargon, Montale calls it, "una parola gergale," Milanese for a stupid fellow, and ratifying Yeats's dictum that the poet must "think like a wise man, yet express himself like the common people." The yield of this expressing, as the hermetic poet poaches on the vernacular, is the simulacrum of everyday speech. Domesticating the winged horse of poetry, "our colt," he brings it down from the "intense inane."

Every great poet has his quarrel with Pegasus. First of all he must establish his independence of the past, "the sublime in the old sense." Already Petrarch, than whom no poet pays more homage to the past, complains that the vein of accustomed skill is dry, "Secca è la vena dell'usato ingegno." The detecting of dryness is often polemical, the new poet aggrandizing his "poesia pura" or "desnuda" or "pur" against the "periphrastic study" of his fathers. I think we feel poetry to be more or less successful as it steers clear of polemicizing and communicates an air of involuntariness. Leopardi is febrile when ideas have got hold of him, and Corazzini and the other "Crepuscular" poets from whom Montale takes his cue are only enacting a program. Sometimes Montale, wringing wine from sour grapes, shares their insufficiency. But in his poetry when it works, you feel that he can do no other.

Lacking "ideas" and having no option, he immerses himself in the corrosive element he lives in. At the same time, he is a panegyrist of the long past. But the sonorities of a poet like Rilke are beyond him. For example, the *Duino Elegies*: "Look, we don't love like flowers, with only a single/ season behind us; immemorial sap/ mounts in our arms when we love." Montale is rarely so impassioned, and you listen in vain for the humming sound, like "a thousand twangling instruments," that summons to apocalypse. From the start, he casts a cold eye on life, on death. But what is left over, the passionate residue of a skeptical spirit—"un filo di pietà"—is more telling as the cold has had its way with the passion.

The passion wanes as the body dies but recurs with each new day, "On wires, on wings, in the wind... at every turning" ("Mottetti XI"). After all Montale is the heir of Leopardi, the quintessential romantic, celebrating the humble broom that flowers on the slopes of the volcano where everything is clinker. The flower, though doomed, has its fragrance, or say that the fragrance is contingent. The sea breaks against the shore, hurling up a spuming cloud. Inevitably the flats reabsorb it. But for an instant the sterile vortex greens and we know ourselves among the living ("I Morti").

Montale's laconic manner, the reticence, and the hermetic strain, are the appropriate face, turned to our inspection, of a coin minted in agony. Affronted by the enormous presence of death, he ventures only a soundless howl, "l'ululo muto" (in "Ballata Scritta in una Clinica"). The agony is real, precluding fulsome speech. "What is he whose grief bears such an emphasis?" Hamlet, hater of hyperbole, asks this question at the grave of Ophelia.

Reading Montale we are apt to think of Dante, but not as an influence. They share a psychology, a stony face, Old Rocky Face. Ugolino, his children dead and dying, doesn't speak or shed a tear. His silence describes the man who has given all there is to give, as he is true to himself and his occasion. Truth to the occasion isn't gracious but acquired. When Juliet in the play bids farewell to poetry, her deliberate want of confecting meets us like a blow. The reticence of Montale is like this.

There is the violence a new convention enjoins on us, as when Auden says it is unbecoming to stink of poetry. We feel this didactic violence in Pound, I think we feel it in Eliot to his demerit, and in some of Montale's early poems where life is shards of broken bottles on the summit of a wall. How tedious, how literary. There is the violence that is psychological, costive or pinched, and sometimes Montale, fishing the dull canal behind the gashouse, betrays it. It is his dismal pleasure. Then there is that meditated violence when the poet chooses his instrument and has the manage of it, bias and intelligence making a conjunction, and it is in this kind that Montale cuts a permanent figure.

In the world of his imagining, dust blows and eddies over roofs and empty spaces: "spiazzi," before the church, whose portals are

closed. Hooded horses sniff the ground and are otherwise immo-
bile ("Arsenio"). Journeying toward this "alien orbit," the poet finds
his way home. Negating is affirming, and the denial of specious
beauty the resuscitating of beauty. These surprises are Montale's
particular mode, not the kernel of his art—a false conceit, that of
the husk and kernel—but a consort of dissimilar voices.

His music is "crepuscular" as it merges things convention keeps
apart, for instance the anti-romantic side and the Leopardi. Though
contemptuous of "New Sirens" and weather-worn Tritons, he carries on the romantic tradition, saluting "the wild fire that burned in
the veins of the world." So two truths are told of Montale, and perhaps this phrase of Shakespeare's holds for all writers of size. Readers
who want to get him straight will seek to run the two together.

Characteristically, his self-portrait says what he isn't and doesn't
want: "cio che *non* siamo, cio che *non* vogliamo." Partly what he
doesn't want is "poetry." "Why do you call me a poet?" Corazzini
inquires:

> Perché tu mi dici: poèta?
> Io non sono un poèta.

Montale, like those "Crepuscolari" or twilight poets, repudiates the
fictive order of boxwood and acanthus, fabricated by "the poets
laureate," a derisive appellation ("I Limoni"). But this is only one
side of him.

On the other he repudiates the disorder of his own time, "forme,
opache, sono sparse," a heap of broken images disposed as by Eliot,
devoid of form and "scattered in a cold repose." Montale in the
Waste Land keeps his solicitude and his memory inviolate. Like
Yeats in his *Mythologies*, he honors parochial business—"what
happened under the thorn-tree forty years ago." His poetry is lower
case and not synoptic but myopic, both its deprivation and success.
He sees no order except as he can tease it from private disorder, the
surf or backwash of memory, "una risacca di memorie," whelming
the heart ("Crisalide"). Asserted orders, imposed by Right or Left—
"chierico rosso, o nero"—are out. The old stridor is out, "lettere di
fuoco," D'Annunzio and his torpedo boat, all that. So are the old
pieties, the cult of "Il Passatismo," Carducci genuflecting before
the past.

But though it has no message, Montale's poetry is political and social, as what great poetry is not. His poetry exacts a full look at the worst, and when he won't blink he commits a political act. But he doesn't want to be counted among the unacknowledged legislators of the world: he prefers the patient labor of taxonomy, finding the exact names of things—quoting Jiminez, "la cosa misma." He can't or won't afford us that heuristic component great poetry is supposed to afford. Listen, I am Lazarus come from the dead, come back to tell you all.

Like Dr. Williams in "The A, B and C of It," he sits to the tutelage of his senses. In "I Limoni": "Time without odor is Time without me." The matter he deals in can't be severed from earth. Always he offers the adverbial qualifier: "ove si lagnano/ i lui nidaci." The garden he evokes in the poem of that title isn't an archetype but an indigenous place. Unfledged wrens lament there. The localizing detail, tying it to earth, annuls the chance for general statement.

That seems to me no great loss. In poetry, not only Montale's, general statements are uninteresting in and for themselves. Montale succeeds, not as he is philosophically persuasive, rather as his poetry, some of it anyway, makes a memorable coherence. It isn't exactly off the point to ask him what he means, but perhaps asking acknowledges the poverty of his accomplishment. If we are lucky, says Stevens, we get to a place where the thing which is the poem yields to a clarity and we observe contentedly, where observing shrinks the world to a palpable whole

> That we do not need to understand, complete
> Without secret arrangements of it in the mind.

The palpable whole is referential—"like warty squashes, streaked and rayed"—but partly it refers to itself. I think I am true to Montale in saying: poetry is the arrow of blood whose bloody course you must certify, and points the way to Aleppo; is recognized as the world tightens, incandescent, in the lava which brings your profane love to Galilee; most of all is never catholic, whatever they tell you in school.

This last is the sense of Mandelstam's Law of Identity. A=A. "The word is Psycheia. The living word does not denote an object"— what you might denote as precisely by employing some other word—but "a thing in all its concreteness." Poetry doesn't communicate intellectual content, not when it is most nearly itself. Our few ideas are common coin and inexpensive, undeserving of notice unless made peculiar by form. The poet, Montale says, is searching for "a precise truth, not for the general truth." Though he sings about that which unites one man to all the rest, he so pitches his music as not to deny, as being unable but to assert "that which distinguishes and differentiates him from others and renders him unique and unrepeatable." Better to say—what I really had rather not say—that in poetry the ideas don't matter, than to lose yourself in the great bog where the intellectual panders are mired, hunting the kernel of thought. In achieved poetry there is no kernel nor any husk that contains it. Dr. Williams, distinguishing the excellence of Pound, has shrewder words than mine: "It is that the material is so molded that it is changed in kind from other statement. It is a *sort* beyond measure."

\* \* \*

Montale's style embodies problems personal to him, and laying them out is the function of criticism. But his style is more imperious than the modern critic's famous "vehicle" on which the message or "tenor" is seated. It dictates the kind of problems that will or can be at issue. Seeking to resolve them, he isn't less energetic than practitioners of the didactic sciences. But such agreement as he achieves is largely emotional, and his resolution is metrical, therefore felicitous.

A more ambitious or less speculative poet resolves experience in a trenchant "clausula": any special cadence that calls attention to itself. The epigram does this. But "Epigram's an assassin," "La Pointe assassine," Verlaine calls it, and Montale settles for memorializing the turbid surface of experience, the scattering of pigs as the auto fords the river, the carillon of the church of San Gusme, a May moon, all staining, so attesting the white radiance or meaningless flux of eternity ("Verso Siena"). His purview is limited, and illumination is reserved to effects, not to causes. Quoting Eliot in *The Rock*: "We see the light that fractures through unquiet water./ We see the light but see not whence it comes."

This isn't a virtue, only characteristic. Like Eliot, Montale is at his wit's end in postulating a necessary cause. The conclusion of *The Waste Land* succumbs to the stony rubbish out of which it grows. Montale, step by step, is often the victim of his material and the imitative form which describes it. In his poetry when it doesn't cash for us, emotion is felt as merely personal, and the blistered rhetoric is vented in air. It seems worth recalling that he translated *Timon of Athens*, one of Shakespeare's least realized plays. He is feeling for affinities.

This aggressive bit of nastiness from *Satura*, Montale's penultimate volume, suggests in the poetry a condition of stasis which approaches morbidity.

> He was not ever seen.
> The rabble, however, waited for Him,
> for the present-arms: overflowing funnels,
> pitchforks and spits, a fetid string
> of saltimbocca. And yet
> not one time did He extend
> His mantle's hem or the point of His crown
> beyond the black and fecal bastions.

The Creator doesn't impinge on us, either for good or evil, and doesn't abide our question. He, or His Creation, is a pig in a poke.

Here are images taken at random from the whole of Montale's work: a sun without heat extinguishing its torches, a black current and dragonflies skimming above it, time regurgitating, barges half submerged and black on the high waves, volcanoes painted on sea shells: the gimcrackery you buy in a fun fair, auto horns like those that signal the approach of Sweeney to Mrs. Porter in the spring. Predictably the spring is dark or comes on like a mole. Summer is the dog days, and in winter the sky looks down myopically on bleached nets drying slowly in a cold light. Nowhere in the poems do we find the source of Montale's anguish. It seems unlocated, like Hardy's, whose poems lamenting the death of his wife were among "the peaks of modern poetry," his translator said. Though the wretchedness they communicate isn't surprising, it was there from the beginning and never goes away. Montale's case is similar. I think we say that the trouble is human beingness but this begs the question, unless you are willing to appeal from this world to another.

How do you find a nomenclature for what cannot be denominated, "this torture without name," or rationalize what isn't open to rationalization, "the event that was not necessary" ("Crisalide")? In "The Hitler Spring" Montale puts the question, "Tutto per nulla, dunque?" "Is it all for nothing, then?" Who is going to respond to him, unless the yea-sayers against whose hand your heart would break, or the professional Jeremiahs who make money from wringing their hands. Montale scrapes his answers, rather his approximations, as he cheats syntactically, for example, in the elegy to Dora Markus where the adjective "invisibile" describes impartially the words that follow and precede it. You can't see the far shore ("sponda") or the heroine's true country ("la tua patria vera"), so are left impaled on the horns of understanding. Or Montale makes an emulsion of contradictory truths: "Derelitte... sfaccetta," the desolation of the living that nonetheless cuts facets in the sun and rain ("Tempi di Bellosguardo"). Life is chill but resplendent but the splendor that declares it is reflected from stone ("Eastbourne"). Or life is the twinning of grace and the inferno ("Mottetti I"). Always two truths confront one another. Neither gets hegemony and neither is denied.

In an untitled poem from his first volume, *Ossi di Seppia* or *Cuttlefish Bones*, Montale presents himself as searching out the evil that bores through the world. He is remembering Virgil in the last canto of the *Inferno*. By such stairs which are the body of Lucifer himself "we must go forth from so much evil." So the poet takes hold "of the hair of the guilty worm that pierces the world" and climbs upward from darkness. That is what Virgil does. Montale, more dogged, stays behind. Or you can put it that his proper element is hebetude and pain. Negotiating our descent to the ninth circle of the Inferno, he leaves us there, where the piano roll music of the damned quickens in tempo, shrilling in the spheres of ice. This music is omnipresent, a cacophonous harmony ("un travolto concitamento d'accordi"), like the "song of screech-owls" or of a "broken harmonica in the darkening day." Malraux's character in *Man's Hope* hears the "Internationale" played by a blind man on his concertina while the final triumph of the Fascists prepareds. The summons to our enfranchisement echoes like a clamor in a vault. (Montale's phrase is "un vuoto risonante.") For Malraux, however, hope is the key, and the music isn't derisory but tragic.

From Montale's music, tragic sonorities are mostly excluded. Riding the carousel, or merry-go-round composed of hours that are pretty much the same, we hear melody that mocks itself, the shuddering of tambourines over the dark pit, a sarabande accompanied by howling. Castanets reiterate a tiresome refrain. A voice in the wind dispenses a lilting air. The verb is incongruous, "dispensare," evoking largesse. But the air is promoted "by the muse or some machine." This is Hell, nor is he out of it.

But remaining in Hell, he engineers our freedom. He is the hateful Jonah, an inauspicious presence we would like to commit to the deep. But Jonah is auspicious too, and ministers to our health. He rubs the gall of a fish on the eyes of a blind man and the white film falls from his eyes. "He flogs and he has mercy, he takes men down to Hades and he brings them up." He is Dante the poet to our Virgil-pilgrim, and like Dante he himself is forbidden access to the kingdom. Against Hades, in fifty years of poetry, he tendered his gratuities—the incorruptible green of the camphor tree, the brief hour of human tremor, the "slow gazing round of eyes that now know how to see." Through his disinterested agency we climb, in Yeats's phrase, "to our proper dark."

In the only ways that count for poetry, Montale is a teaching poet, necessarily kinetic. To say how he moves us is to venture a comment on the physics of poetry. We are transported, but not from poverty to riches or even from unhappiness to its always unlikely opposite. The movement is to a state of mind characterized by vulnerability and openness, and results in a juster measure of life as it might consist. This hypothetical state is where the poet sows his energizing seeds. He doesn't intellectualize, a bad thing to do, but is intelligent or apprehensive.

The warmth of revelation fails to come down to him. Like the early heretic Nestorius, who disbelieves in the Incarnate Word, he is locked in a fire of frost. But declining to accept the Truth we take on faith, perhaps unable to grasp it, he directs attention to the humbler truths we gather from experience. In his world, no bark of salvation rides on the billowing sea "beyond the bars." No Charon waits to ferry us, nor his complement, the angel-pilot of the *Purgatorio*. The bark itself, both real and illusory, figures our adhesion to earth.

"There are instances in which the bottle tossed in the sea finally reaches its destination." Montale is praising the modern French poet René Char, whose poems are a tough nut, even for the most willing reader. "In Char the sudden instant, the moment, swings open its doors and plunges him into the concrete experience of eternity." This gives the sense of Montale's title, *Le Occasioni*. But it stands for all his best poetry, occasions or instances when "the flash of lightning candies the trees and walls and surprises them," dispelling the dark.

# 5

# The Prose of Osip Mandelstam

Osip Mandelstam died more than sixty years ago, unknown to Western readers and a non-person in his own country. Since then his critical stock has gone way up but he remains the possession of a priestly class, Slavicists in universities, mainly American, and the odd practicing poet. Perhaps for this artful dodger that is just as well. "The arts that have escaped best," said Oscar Wilde, who knew what he was talking about, "are the arts in which the public takes no interest." Mandelstam's story suggests how the interest, though prurient, carries with it a superstitious regard. An early inmate of the concentration camp, the non-person feared for his life. His widow Nadezhda reports this in her memoirs, permanent books of our time (*Hope Against Hope*, 1970; *Hope Abandoned*, 1974). "Tell him to calm down," says a condescending warder. "We don't shoot people for making up poetry." In effect, though, they did.

Mandelstam's prose, a prod or refreshment, led him back to poetry when his poetic well had gone dry. For five years, a "deaf-mute" time, he wrote nothing he cared to save, then, in "Fourth Prose," resumed "the role of witness." This got inspiration going again and made possible the poems dated 1930 and later. But the prose, though enabling, is more than "an adjunct to the Muses' diadem" and asks to be read for its own sake. A lot of it survives, almost 600 pages of criticism and letters (trans. Jane Gary Harris and Constance Link, Ann Arbor, 1979). The publisher, Ardis, is America's chief collector and disseminator of samizdat, literature the Soviets would have suppressed, and Carl Proffer, the press's founder, made it his business to thwart them.

A more portable volume (*The Noise of Time*, ed. and trans. Clarence Brown, San Francisco, North Point Press, 1986), mines this rich lode and supplements it with other work. It has four of the five major pieces: the title essay, vignettes of St. Petersburg; a surrealistic novella, "The Egyptian Stamp," also autobiographical, though this isn't apparent on a first reading; "Journey to Armenia," travel literature telling of exotic places, not all on the map; and "Fourth Prose," a cry from the heart when Mandelstam must have known they were coming to get him. Not collected is his sending up of belletristic criticism, "Conversations About Dante." Aphoristic and implacably épater-le-bourgeois, i.e., anti-new Soviet man, this late essay pays homage to the poet as exile. "Fantastic homelessness" was Mandelstam's lot, and partly he is looking in the mirror. Pinpointing Dante's greatness, he says what poetry is and isn't. It isn't ideas, as when we fillet out the meaning or message. "For where there is amenability to paraphrase, there the sheets have never been rumpled, there poetry... has never spent the night." Mandelstam wrote this in a time when the word was sacrosanct, not the Word Made Flesh but pronouncements on billboards.

Like certain other twentieth-century writers—"daedalian" Joyce or Montale under the Fascists—he presents the outsider. Between him and society a state of war exists, but the blame doesn't lie with the Communists, who have enough sins on their head. Mandelstam's quarrel with society transcends ideology, something ideologues don't understand. Essentially a man of honor, he was his brother's keeper. Cain the first murderer who rejected this role turns up often in Mandelstam's pages, minus the hangman's hands. A pillar of society, he chooses for acquaintance "people no more offensive than the croutons in his bouillon" or shuts the door in your face if you jeopardize his business, "untouched by any shame since 1881." Meanwhile Mandelstam, beset by fellow feeling, bearded the lion in his den. Clarence Brown's biography (1973) tells how he protested the death warrants drawn up by a henchman of "Iron Felix" Dzerzhinsky, Lenin's chief of secret police. He wasn't the stuff conventional heroes are made of—trips to the dentist reduced him to panic—and would have shunned this devoir gladly but couldn't.

Descended on his father's side from German speakers on the Baltic, Mandelstam was born in Warsaw, January 15, 1891. He grew up in St. Petersburg, an elegant city dreamed by a westernizing tsar, in Russia, not of it. Moscow, brick-colored and watermelon-empty, stood for the real Russia. Later, when Mandelstam became famous or notorious, Communist Party reviewers put an unerring finger on his apartness. One review is headed bitterly, "Shades of Old Petersburg." Where else would this stuck-up poet have come from?

His boyish sympathies were Marxist, not theoretical but part of the fellow feeling, and mostly his socialism is a cry of pain. He tossed *Das Kapital* aside; "the same," he said disgustedly, "as Kraevich's Physics." He didn't "hear" abstract concepts--too mellifluous, maybe, for a considering ear—and preferred the "true historical dissonance." At school, geography, an agreeable hodgepodge ("puffing away at a pipeful of Capstan tobacco"), turned into anecdotes about American trusts. Populating the visible world with Jacob's ladders, the young Marxist-with-a-difference sent small and large property holders up and down the rungs, "passing through the stages of capitalist economy." No doubt Marxism has more claim on our attention than this, but there seems a kind of temperament that can't cope with the Logos until it puts on flesh. This temperament is Mandelstam's, and out of fashion with the doyens of thought in our time.

As a young man he traveled in Western Europe, studied at Heidelberg (Old French), then at St. Petersburg University. He was only a middling student and took no degrees, being about his father's business, not the leather merchant's, his father in heaven. This involved poetry, a disinterested activity that didn't help set the table. A first book, *Stone*, appeared in 1913, published at his own expense. By then the young maître was sporting side-whiskers à la Pushkin. He is clean-shaven, though, in a drawing made two years later, and looks like a haughtier and younger version of Whistler's Mother. He invited satire, and that was how the artist, P.V. Miturich, meant us to see him.

In 1920 a would-be poet sought a verdict on his poems from this severe and passionate arbiter. "It was important to him that I cease writing poetry, and his words were a defense of poetry against me and those dozens and hundreds of young men and women who were busying themselves with the game of words." A harsh verdict, Mandelstam's suggests a young man as unselfconscious as those others he was raging against. But more than this it argues total commitment, the kind that pitiless Christ enjoins on a sentimental disciple. Poetry was a game but played for mortal stakes. He called it a luxury, also vital, and sometimes bitter like their Russian bread.

Aggravating his outsider's role, the cosmopolitan poet was Jewish. In the beginning he shied from "the chaos of Judaism," but getting older flaunted "the honorable title of Jew," insisting on his inheritance from sheep breeders and patriarchs. His Jewish blood rebelled against the "gypsies" who plied the writing trade. He wasn't born from hucksters' loins. Just into his twenties, he had himself baptized a Christian. Some think this step expedient, a Jew escaping the heat, but if that is true it was out of the frying pan and into the fire, and in a bad time for religion he took his personal brand of Christianity to heart. The writing proclaims this, for example an essay of 1921: "The Christian—and every cultivated man is a Christian now—knows not a metaphysical hunger or a merely spiritual nourishment. For him, the word is also flesh, and simple bread is happiness and mystery."

Mandelstam's life is an alphabet of woes but his art is happy. In the years of his adulthood, morose bearded men browbeat the Russian people, slow-witted students in their murderous classroom where the walls were damp with fear. Is not Lenin the spit and image of the schoolmaster type? Against the didactic men, Mandelstam's weapon is play. Forecasting the Bolsheviks, intellectuals in Russia took a dim view of this. With them "it was always Lent." Acquainted with shadows, he sought to disperse them. His writing makes a setoff to his life, and in it he kept a perpetual Shrovetide. "Hooray for the living!" This cry (from "Journey to Armenia") echoes in the writing. He said that Linnaeus, the eighteenth-century botanist and one of his heroes, "managed his task with dexterity and gaiety, like a barber shaving the Burgermeister, or a Dutch housewife grinding coffee on her lap in a fat coffee mill." The whimsical portrait gives his likeness, completing the one of him as Whistler's Mother.

Chary of pronouncements, he ventured them sometimes. Soon after Russia entered the First World War, he defined the goal of our two-thousand-year-old culture as a release into freedom. That sounded like the old millenarian rag and eschatologists pricked up their ears. Then this Groucho, flicking his cigar ash, told them that freedom wasn't for salvation's sake but all "for the sake of play." Making things worse, he traced it "to the miraculous mercy of Christianity." His brand of Christianity doesn't address itself to heaven, however, much less to building heaven on earth. It turned us loose to play in the fields of the Lord.

Disappointing the pietists and social activists alike, Mandelstam peddled no doctrine. His prose is fiercely doctrinal, however—but the end is "spiritual joy." Dante, his model poet, comments obliquely. In the famous letter to his patron, Can Grande della Scala, he gives us the poetics that form up the *Commedia*, written, he says, "not for the sake of speculative philosophy but for the sake of practical needs." Like Mandelstam, Dante is having his joke on the bearded men, and his practical business is "to remove those living in this life from a state of misery and to guide them to a state of happiness." The business isn't doable in blue books, but transacted in the livelier milieu of art. Mandelstam illustrates by referring readers to Manet and Monet, a temple of air, light, and glory.

Forward-looking contemporaries wanted to knock down the temple and build a new city on its ruins. Allowing them their eleemosynary impulse, Mandelstam's widow says he was made a sacrifice to "the inverted humanism of the times." Humanism in the root sense means bettering the lot of the many, and he felt the urgency of this. Generous men like him pulled the wool over their eyes, unbidden. Russia's new rulers, Mme. Mandelstam thought, could have dispensed with prisons and capital punishment. "My desire is not to speak about myself," he assured them, aware that "I" had suddenly become non grata. Trying to establish credentials, he wrote darkly of some modern art "because it is a world in itself." Much pathos in this, telling of an ardent spirit for whom "Comrade" was a lovely name. Afraid that the Revolution might pass him by, he took his place with the others in the terrifying, patient line creeping toward the yellow window of the box office. This was where they gave out tickets to the future.

But he knew that one of these days they would come to throw him out—out of the Society of the Last Word and the Circle for Grasshopper Music. He prayed that this might not happen but made sure it did. "Molecular" he was, breaking down things like the Flaubert he belittled and any writer worth reading. His prose, though hardly ego-centered, opens one man's window on the world. Poking his head out, he breathed "stolen air." Other metaphors of his signal the troublemaker. While around him the bitch pack "wrote," a mechanical activity like producing sounds from a phonograph needle, he alone worked "from the voice." "I am a Chinaman," he said, "no one understands me." What sort of pineapple was this, they wondered, forever dodging what he was supposed to do. He never quite figured out an answer, knowing only that when the "tin subpoena" came, demanding that he cease his skullduggery and promise not to travel beyond certain specific limits, he would agree on the spot—but immediately start dodging all over again.

Supporting himself by literary hackwork, including translations, he negotiated the post-Revolutionary decade, still (in Akhmatova's phrase) "relatively vegetarian." Nineteen twenty-eight saw a collected edition of his poems and prose. But enemies, baying his stag, accused him of plagiarizing in one of the translations. Remembering Dante, he said he was stopped "midway on the path of life... in the dense Soviet forest by bandits who called themselves my judges." Interrogations followed, increasingly sinister, and only the intervention of Nikolai Bukharin, a member of the Politburo, saved his neck. Regret is the fruit of pity, said one of the Mongol conquerors of Russia, and later Bukharin died in Stalin's Great Purge, the same year as Mandelstam.

A healthy child of sickness, "Fourth Prose" is his response to the bandits. Written in the winter of 1929, it remained unpublished until 1966, not in the Soviet Union. Mandelstam knew it wouldn't be published and knew this about much of his work. Once in Petersburg he recited some new poems—sang them, said a dazzled member of the audience, "like a shaman seized by visions." (Brodsky, "singing" his poems, is of the tribe of Mandelstam.) When could the audience expect to see the poetry in print? "Not now, at least," he said. "A time of silence is coming." How can a man write if no one is reading him? He revolved this question, the most poignant of all for a writer, and thinking about the Commedia said that Dante meant it to be "the property of a time as yet unborn but already indebted."

His laconic title, "Fourth Prose," was private shorthand, said Nadezhda Mandelstam. It designated his fourth piece of prose, "but there was also an association with the 'fourth estate' which so much preoccupied him, as well as with our 'Fourth Rome.'" The first three estates, coming down from feudal times, included the nobility, clergy, and commons. Writers, unacknowledged legislators, made up the fourth. Russia was the Third Rome, after Rome itself and Constantinople. "More resplendent than the sun," it laid down the law to all nations. "For two Romes have fallen," said a fifteenth-century monk of Pskov, "but the Third stands, and a Fourth shall never be." Mandelstam thought otherwise, and his entire career can be read as a vindication of the Fourth Rome, not yet established but waiting its time. "I want to live in the imperative of the future passive participle," he said, "in the 'what ought to be.'"

Reprieved from the bandits and sent to Armenia by his friend in power, he was supposed to write a perky travel piece on life in this Socialist republic. The result was "Journey to Armenia," a hymn to light against darkness, though just at present the light has been doused. It ends with a prose poem that seems to glance at Stalin's tyranny. That was how the censor read it, and the magazine editor who ran this equivocal celebration found himself out of a job. Afterwards, Mandelstam didn't get published.

In 1934 at a small gathering of friends, probably in Pasternak's apartment, he read an epigram on Stalin, "the Kremlin highlander" whose thick fingers were fat like worms. One of the friends whispered to the police, and Mandelstam drew three years in exile. He had a brief respite after his release but they picked him up again, May 1, 1938. The charge was counterrevolutionary activity and the sentence five years. This time, making sure, they sent him to a "corrective labor camp" in the East, five thousand miles from Moscow. In his incarceration, "totally exhausted, terribly thin, almost unrecognizable," he verged on madness. His last letter is lucid, however. It reports his expectation of being "sent from this place" but adds, "I apparently got 'sifted out' and will have to get ready for the winter." He didn't make it through the winter and died, still in his forties, near Vladivostok, on or about December 27, 1938.

\*   \*   \*

This matter of fact ballasts his prose, all of it personal but at a remove from his life. Like the poetry, the prose says one thing in terms of another. Partly that is Aesopian cunning, a writer's refuge against the censor, but also modern-hermetic. Mandelstam, a good modern, doesn't care to put his cards on the table, not from timidity but fastidiousness. Profoundly an economist, he hated leftover things, and reading him you look in vain for guidons. How they spoil the comeliness of writing, sticking out all over it like doodads. "Thus we see." "Moreover." "Indeed." This "snow leopard" who was one of a kind and lived in an unspeakable time and place is true to his artist-contemporaries across the European and American spectrum. It is extraordinary how, without intention, they echo each other. R. P. Blackmur, who called himself the Double Agent, seems to echo Mandelstam, "a double dealer, with a double soul."

"The Egyptian Stamp," an improbable fiction, has for its setting Petersburg in the "Kerensky Summer" between the two revolutions of 1917. But the setting is out of di Chirico, nightmarish vistas, and though this fiction allows itself a plot or rather two plots, linear it isn't. Parnok, a meager hero standing in for the author, tries to get the tailor to give him his clothes back. Also he tries and fails to prevent the lynching of a little man accused of stealing a watch. Hateful to the mob, this man is the thief of time and indifferent to "the mottoes on sundials." Two narratives, then, but they don't connect, and mostly Mandelstam's novella is a series of discrete-seeming pictures flashing in uncertain sequence past the eye. This technique is like Eliot's (after Pound's blue pencilling), reducing *The Waste Land* to its essentials. The essentials look like shards, though.

Fragmenting the big picture, Mandelstam does the same with its component parts. A passage from "The Egyptian Stamp" suggests (in negative ways) what he is up to:

> The railroad has changed the whole course, the whole structure, the whole rhythm of our prose. It has delivered it over to the senseless muttering of the French *moujik* out of Anna Karenina. Railroad prose... is full of the coupler's tools, delirious particles, grappling-iron prepositions, and belongs rather among things submitted in legal evidence.

Meanly expository, this prose bores us to death (him anyway). Mandelstam, resisting it, gets rid of the ligatures. Words like "moreover" never sully his lips. "I write," you hear him saying, "let the reader read."

A credentialed modern both as Symbolist and Acmeist and under whatever label, he paid his respects to "Mother Philology," in nothing placable. "Philia" plus "logos" = love of the word. This makes him a highbrow writer, the only kind worth having, and uncongenial to "moujiks" in all countries. His mother's speech was

Great Russian, his father's he called tongue-tie, that of an autodidact fighting his way out of the Talmudic wilderness. "Somewhere in the vicinity" Spinoza was breeding his spiders in a jar. From the confluence of these tongues his own took its being. He has it "feeding" on its sources like an avid, living thing, or "composing" itself like an artist. Most, indifferent to language, leave their bones in the wilderness. Mandelstam, the wretched life notwithstanding, should be seen as a survivor, the man who came through.

His lingua franca, reflecting its mixed provenance, smells of books and study. This is the reverse of pedantic, i.e. inert, and the books, palpable and sentient, also dynamic, nourished his writing. Describing them, he imagined people, "chubby little butterballs," "soldiers in flying battalions." Books put him in possession of amazing energies. (One of them, not moribund but quick, "lay like someone alive" in the narrow coffin of the age.) This made him a man to reckon with, and speaking for the subversive brotherhood of artists he said that a page of music—or, we can say, a stanza of verse—was a revolution in an ancient German city. In a sense unsuspected by social engineers, his art is revolutionary. The change it heralds begins at home, though. Par excellence the cultivated man, he accommodated modern times, the Enlightenment, and the Middle Ages, and like a learned friend of his, felt the centuries as he felt the weather. ("What a nice century we're having!") Some literary professors in the time before our know-nothing age know as much as he did, but lack his passionate hospitality.

His early poetry is Symbolist, meaning partly inchoate, but by 1913 he was honoring the rose (for example) for its petals and smell, leaving aside the mystical penumbra. This is like Yeats, offloading the dreamy cargo that stuffs his first books, and moving on in just these years to "The Green Helmet" (1910). But putting it that way is apt to sow confusion, the old one between content and form. Worse than birdy babbling by the brook is no-speak where "content" is everything and the form, a loose-leaf binder, contains it. Mandelstam recognized his enemies (not all of them Communists) when he came upon them reading Pushkin in Esperanto. Now that was sinister!

Introducing an English translation of his poetry (1977), Mme. Mandelstam recalls him saying "that the contents are squeezed from the form as water from a sponge." There speaks the modern hero.

Emphasizing content, the message-mongers came up dry, a villain's just deserts. Anyway, as strong men know, the more potent, the more yielding, and "The signal waves of meaning vanish, having completed their work." What Mandelstam liked best about the doughnut was the hole. For real work he had a figure, Brussels lace. "The main thing in it is what holds the pattern up: air, punctures, truancy." In the Dante essay he estimated the role of the "music," by which we want to understand all those adventitious things that go under the name of style. Like a simile of Dante's, confessing no debt to some beggarly logical necessity, it "operates in direct proportion to our ability to do without it."

This is a paradox, for style is the essential thing, a genuine writer's nearest and dearest. "Not merely a guest invited to step indoors," it makes "a full participant in the argument." Logically off the point, "it promotes the exchange of opinions, coordinates it, and encourages syllogistic digestion, stretches premises and compresses conclusions." Centripetal in their tendency, the comrades and their fellow travelers (bankers, lawyers, and captains of erudition) want to come to the point. Like Dante he could have told them that the point, if worth taking, is circumferential.

"What is to be done?" said Lenin, after the hapless critic and would-be novelist Chernyshevsky (just the wrong question for a novelist to pose). Of course Lenin stayed for an answer, labored and "contractual." Never mind the vulgar misunderstanding: Mandelstam set his chisel to a harder stone. His subjects are the big ones: "Insomnia. Homer. Taut sails," less tractable, all of them, than Lenin's NEP. In "Journey to Armenia" he makes room for a Party hack who adorned the Russian Association of Proletarian Writers. A Party member first and only then a poet, he was "the strongman who lifts cardboard weights." Stone is a good generic title for Mandelstam, and in the end the weights he carried broke his back. Until then, he showed much physical prowess.

Poetry needed this prowess and began with going out on the roads. "In all seriousness" he canvassed the question: "how many shoe soles, how many oxhide soles, how many sandals did Alighieri wear out during the course of his poetic work, wandering the goat paths of Italy." Mandelstam's prose is very much a poet's, that is, intensely masculine in its feeling for thingness. Words were like building blocks, each with its poise or heft, and the writer, deploying them, is like a master builder. Architecture was the demon that kept him company, and he looked for its rudiments in objects and the words that bodied them forth. Pinecones were Gothic and acorns hypocritical in their monastic caps. Illustrious men, his familiars, lend glamour to the prose, but humble men who work with their hands suggest him better. (Writing is work for hands, a reason to stick to pencil or pen.) There was that old Sergeev who made the tall red bookcases in the zoology library. This carpenter could name the wood of already finished lumber, whether oak, ash, or pine, by rubbing his palm over it, eyes closed.

Sometimes a macaroni (but only spoilsports will mind), Mandelstam liked words for their own sake and liked shoving them around until they made a composition. In Armenia, his ideal country where everyone was his own philologist, they jangled the keys of language even when there weren't any treasures to unlock. His prose that calls attention to itself does this too. Often, cocking an ear, it listens for echoes, and his translator notices how the second word in a sequence is apt to be the "phonic shadow" of the first. Words were potent like spells, their quality not exhausted in dictionary meanings. Reading Symbolist poetry involved him in a thicket of *shch* sounds. Unlike concepts, they came through to the ear.

Before time was, concepts deferred to "apprehensions" (what you apprehend you take hold of, the point to having a prehensile thumb), and all the meanings implicit in seeing, hearing, and understanding coalesced in one semantic bundle. By and by they teased the concept "head" out of their foggy bundle of meanings. "Its symbol became... deafness." His function was to cure it in prose that is good for what ails us. "A plant is a sound," if only we listened, "an event, a happening, an arrow, and not a boring, bearded development."

"Bearded" brings up Father Marx, famous for materialism but essentially a prince of abstracters. The Mandelstam who couldn't read him wasn't anti-intellectual, only hostile to intellectualizing, and meant to reclaim words on their physical side. Coming up from the viscera, they made what Blackmur called a hymn in the throat. The self-conscious prose is partly a manifesto, defending the flesh against abstraction and the void. Like Wallace Stevens, another dandy of language, he thought the greatest poverty was to live in a non-physical world.

Often incongruous, his figures of speech align him with other salvage workers in the modern period. Montale is one, an adept of ugliness who thinks that if you want to resuscitate beauty, you will need to know first what it isn't. Like all good "new" writers, fed up with the proximate past, Mandelstam makes identities of opposites-by-convention, detecting resemblances we hadn't noticed before. Here are some samples, culled at random from the prose: sprouting bayonets like ears of corn, the schoolgirl shyness of apple trees, public telephones as terrifying as the pincers of a crawfish, the raspberry globes of pharmacies, linden trees frightful in their governmental thickness, blue policemanly phizzes of giant trout preserved in alcohol. Concreteness drags this prose earthwards, and readers who like their truth conceptual, "pinnacled dim in the intense inane," will close the book. For such, generalizing always waits at the door.

The trout that suggest policemen come up again, and unexpectedly a Petersburger, attending a concert, is like them. This "feverish little trout" makes his way to "the marble ice-hole of the vestibule." Mandelstam's figures, though surprising, are decorous, and against the frenzy of the crowd is the "Alpine cold" of the performance. In his lavish expense of tropes, teaching or "kinetics" aren't uppermost, however, as when the writer wants to clarify or move you from A to B. This is what metaphors are understood to do. But wouldn't you know it, "a metaphor can only be defined metaphorically." Devoted to appearances like all civilized men, Mandelstam does his best to clarify the thing itself (not the same as the *ding an sich*). But though his presented things have their analogies they suggest other things, not a concept. In an early essay, "The Morning of Acmeism," he offers an equation plus an observation: "A = A: what a magnificent theme for poetry!"

His lapsing in particulars, like his tautologies, if that is what they are, enacts a temperamental bias. His "little book" (he means "Journey to Armenia" but any of the titles will do) "tells us that the eye is an instrument of thought." A taxonomer like Linnaeus painting outlandish monkeys, he prefers being to thinking about it. The images that enliven his prose invite classification, and his translator, disposing them, says how some import life, others death. But import takes a back seat to an animizing imagination, generous like God's on the morning of Creation. Perhaps Mandelstam is generous to a fault.

Always acute but in last things non-judgmental, his essays and fictions confess an artist's impulse to bestow the gift of life. Celebrating François Villon, he said that this poet "managed to combine in one person both plaintiff and defendant." That is the nub of the totalitarian's quarrel with the artist. He doesn't take a stand or rather he stands for everything, and at his animizing touch even the non-human comes to attention. There is the epileptic engine he hears in Armenia. Warmed by mechanics, it mutters a tongue twister, "Not Peter not Helena," as if reporting to Comrade K., former chairman of the Central Executive Committee. The "as if" phrase seems loaded with menace but this comrade is no villain, and boredom has planted fat kisses on his cheeks. That the cheeks are ruddy seems worth noting.

A provincial writer, Mandelstam gets plenty of satisfaction from his lower-case world, "the whole massif of Petersburg," including one small grocery store. The provincialism limits him, though, and he doesn't remove his "argument" to a higher plane. This kind of sensibility is content when "there" turns out to be "here" (Wallace Stevens in his little poem "Crude Foyer"). But "there" is where the conceptualizers hope to take us. Prose that won't let them do that, Mandelstam's, makes a political statement.

Remembering, a conscious act performed in and against a deracinating time, is part of this statement, and though some call it ossifying, appropriate to ageing, he knew it for a "phenomenon of growth." Plough the past under and start again from scratch, they said. Down among the dead men, he foiled them. When very young, he went with his mother to view the embalmed body of the Italian ambassador, dead in the capital and lying in state. He remembered the chocolate building, the black velvet drapings, smell of resin and incense, a glint of silver and tropical plants. "What had all that to do with me?" Verifying the past, it keeps him alive to the present. What had the madeleine to do with Proust?

Childhood meant smells, the "sweetish Jewish smell" that swaddled him in his grandparents' house in German Riga, different from the smell of Aryan houses, or the penetrating smell of tanned leather, evoking his father and identified by the grown man as the smell of the yoke of labor. Things past "tickled his nostrils like a shipment of fresh Kyakhta teas." A house was a full cup, brimful of pastness, and on the walls he hung the "masks" of other men's voices. Never mind what they said; it was enough that he recalled them.

\*  \*  \*

Of course he had to be killed. Dwelling in memory and invigorated by it, he threatened the new men who thought history was beginning tomorrow. To remember was to make your way alone back up the dried riverbed. Oddly, that was how you arrived in the present. "Who were your people?" asks one of the damned in Dante's Inferno. This question reverberates in Mandelstam's prose. Unlike Tolstoy, he didn't ransack the family archives but he wanted to know where he came from, an index of where he might go. It wasn't genealogy that engaged him but continuity, the antonym of chaos.

For all the "melee" of pastness, Petersburg was responsible, most of all for her poor son. "You, Petersburg," he said, "will answer!" Receiving back the streets and squares of the city in the form of galley proofs, he "composed" the prospects, heightening and toning down at need. Melee no more, his city made an order, not screwed down like the new order but bursting with vitality like a work of art. In a time of the breaking of nations, this was a writer's job.

As "The Egyptian Stamp" begins, a cold white flame has been licking for thirty years at the backs of mirrors. "Nothing is left." But he was the keeper of the muniments room and survival depended on him. Outside, the spectators implored him to jump but he couldn't tear himself away from his "dear Egypt of objects," so, risking the fire, saved the past for the future. Montale, acquisitive and tentacular, does this too, Yeats also, who made his peace with learned Italian things, and Eliot, shoring fragments against his ruin.

Imitating the past, Fascists in Rome and Communists in Moscow sought to inter it. Mussolini's Foro Italico is to the Forum as iron pyrite to gold, and Stalin Gothic to Gothic as death is to life. Mandelstam, discriminating, entered his lively protest in time capsules, awaiting the future. Sometimes, going underground or going into the wilderness, he disappeared for weeks on end "in the latifundia of his exemplary world." Call this world "Armenia," the secret place, long desired, where he lived in the mind. Of his mythical Armenia he wouldn't stop dreaming, not couldn't but wouldn't, a defiant act of will. There, if luck held, he might put off his "hooflike" shoes, the mark of the beast they were hunting. Escaping pursuit, the salamander had this luck. It took color from the sand or the paper in the terrarium. But Man, "the thinking salamander," though he could guess tomorrow's weather, couldn't choose his own coloration.

In the real Armenia, Mandelstam journeyed back and forth across the country, savoring it all. One night he lay in Ashtarak, in the village hotel. Kulaks, dispossessed men and women, used to live in the hotel, in other times a private dwelling. Outside his bedroom, the orchard was a dancing class for trees. "Look at their quadrilles." But the day turned stormy. Rain, drenching the mountains, fell in the town. His senses aroused, he listened to the water running in the gutters and ringing and welling up "on all the stories and stands of Ashtarak." This allowed the camel to pass through the eye of the needle.

# 6

# Edwin Muir's Other Eden

T. S. Eliot, patting Edwin Muir and Scotland on the head, said Muir was among the poets Scotland should always be proud of. On the other hand, there hadn't been many. Muir, however, said harsh things about Scotland. He saw it emptied of itself after the Act of Union (1707), and called Burns and Scott "sham bards of a sham nation." "Annie Laurie" made him sick. But he much loved the world, and his last volume is called "One Foot in Eden." As titles go, it seems a little winsome. Muir's Eden includes the serpent, though. That was how you knew it for Paradise, said John Donne.

A moral man, as Scots are apt to be, Muir was also a Christian Socialist who appealed to a world outside history. But his understanding of how we must carry ourselves as we hope for salvation shuttles back and forth between Christian and natural readings. Sometimes he thought "There's better gospel in man's natural tongue" ("The Incarnate One"). Surprising us, his Christian God doesn't intervene in history, as often in past times when His "red right hand" was raised to smite the wicked. History, however, was almost the "march of," and like the Marxists he detested, he supposed you couldn't do much about it.

Offending contemporaries who hoped the see the lion flag fly again over Edinburgh Castle, he cited the ancient language of Scotland, irretrievably lost. Union with England had destroyed it, "the end of an auld sang," said a Scottish patriot, Fletcher of Saltoun. Muir acquiesced in what he felt unable to change. Deferring to history, in contrast to Hugh MacDiarmid, his mighty opposite, he looks disappointingly passive. But that doesn't square with the polemical writer who waded in with his mitts up. A line from an early poem suggests the tension that holds his poetry together: "He builds in faith and doubt his shaking house" ("The Mythical Journey").

Poetry like his, affirming a faith not beholden to reason, seems a bad joke to post-Christians. But his religion, neither ecstatic nor doctrinal, doesn't insist. Like Wordsworth, he had intimations of something beyond him. Whether or not he believed in heaven, he doesn't land us up there, and always, as his poems end, *The road leads on"* ("The Way"). In a long poem, "The Journey Back," his hero, a type of Mankind, walks out into the sun,

> Not knowing the resurrection and the life,
> Shut in his simple recurring day,
> Familiar happiness and ordinary pain.
> And while he lives content with child and wife
> A million leaves, a million destinies fall,
> And over and over again
> The red rose blooms and moulders by the wall.

The last line reads a little like poetry, pejorative sense, but the others are very assured. Partly the assurance comes from Muir's conviction, not what you would expect of a man with his eye on heaven, that the journey counts more than its end.

His activist's conscience, predicable of a Scot, isn't the modern liberal kind that makes society both our crutch and principal culprit. He thought society sinned against the coal miner, who couldn't live a civilized life, while the stockbroker, who wouldn't, sinned against society. His youth died in the slums of Glasgow, and the recollection still brims with outrage. If he were merely sincere, no one would listen to him. His sorrows are turned to account as poetry, though, and like Keats's April shroud in the "Ode on Melancholy," make us happy.

All this is Scots, the sadness that goes with being Celtic and the rare elation that crosses it, the way the warp is crossed by the woof. When the two-in-one thing is working in him, he is a great poet, in "The Brothers," for instance, a poem from the last years of his life:

> Last night I watched my brothers play,
> The gentle and the reckless one,
> In a field two yards away.
> For half a century they were gone
> Beyond the other side of care....

> I thought, How could I be so dull,
> Twenty thousand days ago,
> Not to see they were beautiful.

Sadness fills this poem up, but breaks on the heart like a sunrise.

Though Muir's "seven years Eden" ended in boyhood, his "holy" Celtic forebears, one a priest, stayed with him. (Not all priests in those days were celibate.) Invoking the ancestors helped him get through a life. Here are lines from his deepest place:

> Seek the beginnings, learn from whence you came,
> And know the various earth of which you are made.
>
> ("The Journey Back")

When Scots in the older time stood on Culloden's field, waiting for the cry of "Claymore!" they found their courage by telling themselves where they came from. "I am Alexander," they said, "son of Russell, son of Roger." In our time when parthenogenesis is in again, Muir's counsels will likely fall on deaf ears. This is a pity, for some are worth latching on to.

The poems he wrote over half a century are survivors' work, like the nest the birds build at the end of Yeats's "Tower," or the saving things in "The Waste Land" shored against the poet's ruin. The world looks bleak when you strip it to bedrock, and Muir, taking thought, lets its gratuities be. His poems derive from that "impulse which makes people create a little world around them to which they can attach their affections." He said this in his *Autobiography* {1954), useful reading for millenarians in a hurry to lighten ship and get on to the future.

His entrance into poetry was difficult. He came to it late and was perhaps too much an ideational man. He himself thought this a part of being Scots. "To be serious about poetry is to be not serious enough," said Alastair Fowler, whose admiration for Muir is temperate. Something was missing in him, what Marianne Moore called "all that fiddle." A proneness to abstraction is in all his work, including the prose. Maybe this drew him to Kafka, whose novels he and his wife rendered in English. He has his "own true fire," Ben Jonson's phrase, but too much smoke mingles with it, and a lot of him is quotidian. Some seventeenth-century poets are like that. Bishop Henry King wrote two poems we remember, enough to glorify a lifetime. Turning pages in the Collected Muir, I cull about twenty-five.

John Haines, introducing a new edition of the criticism (The Estate of Poetry, 1962), put it on a par with Eliot's, but he isn't in the same class as a critic, not particular enough, seeing no need. Pattern and Archetype bemuse him, he thinks they sustain him, and in many poems he takes us on a backwards journey, resuming the life of Everyman. In the first version of his autobiography, *The Story and the Fable*, he sees one man, i.e., himself, enacting all the past, something like ontogeny recapitulating phylogeny. This perception is merely personal, so of less account than he thinks it. It cashes for him, however, in poems of reminiscence when the personal experience is so idiosyncratic, that is, personal plus molten, that we are able to make it our own.

Taking us aback, he confesses that under his smiling sea, killers gorge and play ("The Face"). He doesn't come out and name them, and the anxieties that weigh on his mind are free-floating. Often in the poetry they coalesce as "Demon Time," the Trojan War, and the Fall in the Garden. You can subsume all three under his observation that "A crack ran through our hearthstone long ago" ("The Refugees"). All of us are captive to a few images that stamp themselves on our consciousness in earliest childhood. Emergent in the life, they die with it, leaving no trace. For a poet, however, the images that declare him live on in the work, sometimes lighting up its dark places. This is true of Muir.

Time the devourer has haunted many poets, and you could say that Muir, evoking its image, is walking a conventional path. But his revulsion, like Shakespeare's in the Sonnets, seems more than formal. The premature deaths of so many who were close to him, beyond that the violating of Scotland, first by the Sassenach, later by the Industrial Age, bass the old *tempus edax rerum* music. Over and again he writes of betrayal and grievous, though unspecified, loss. But the never-healing wound doesn't fester, and out of it the poetry comes.

His obsession with guilt is an old story nowadays, but he isn't a hand-wringing poet. A veteran of something—rolling up his sleeve, he could show you the scars—he resembles Ulysses on the long voyage home. "All the world was strange/ After ten years of Troy" ("The Return of the Greeks"). Like the Ancient Mariner's, his obsessions grow a little tiresome. Why can't he pull himself together? Creon asks Oedipus the same question.

He could always do the short-line, almost gnomic poem. "Betrayal," from his first book, is one such and likely to last:

> For still she smiles, and does not know
> Her feet are in the snaring lime.
> He who entrapped her long ago,
> And kills her, is unpitying Time.

Here the form is octosyllabic, elsewhere a three-foot line. Neither lends itself to discursive poetry. Rhyme is insistent and might be facile, but is often deliberately skewed. Metrically, Muir is a conservative among modern poets, not an innovator like Eliot. Probably this knocks a few points off his score.

Time's predations energize some of the best of him, like these lines from "The Commemoration":

> Material things will pass
> And we have seen the flower
> And the slow falling tower
> Lie gently in the grass.

Affronted by entropy in personal ways—that is how I hear the mesmerizing rhythms and the terseness, like epitaphs—he "hypostatizes" a more enduring world. "See eld's frosted hair/ Burn black again," and "the dead world grow green." High stakes are apparent in poems like "The Solitary Journey" and "The Mountains." Forced to bear witness, he gains in intensity. Whatever "traumas" afflict him, his readers are the legatees. Of course the hypostatizing—stabbing the concrete into his figure, so putting it before us—had better persuade.

James Shirley, an old poet, has a marvelous poem that chronicles time's triumph. Asking himself how to dispute it, he ends with a parsimonious couplet:

> Only the actions of the just
> Smell sweet and blossom in their dust.

Muir, ending "The Commemoration" is like that, tightfisted and remarkably precise, even for poets. He has to be both, considering the tricky nature of his material, always apt to play the poet false.

"Invisible virtue" is his stay against time, expanding on the air,

> Although no fruit appear
> Nor weight bend down the bough.

This may strike some as pietistic, perhaps less what we feel than "what we ought to say." But bearing out virtue against invincible time takes courage, great suavity too. Contrary to what is generally said, to "tell it slant" is easy, compared to putting your cards on the table. Muir, not shying from declarative statement, embodies what lasts in a figure.

> How can one thing remain
> Except the invisible,
> The echo of a bell
> Long rusted in the rain?

The first two lines, though cast in the form of a rhetorical question, make a statement whose truth isn't easily apparent. The figure validates it, though, moving far from the tangible, not quitting it entirely. Donne does that in his famous figure from the "Valediction Forbidding Mourning." Close-knit souls, though they separate, don't break apart, he says, but endure an expansion, like "gold to airy thinness beat." This gift of distinguishing impalpable things is special to Muir and not often encountered since the seventeenth century.

*    *    *

But I want to cast in relief my sense of why he will last. More than any other modern poet I know, he repossesses for us the lost place back in the beginning. Great pathos enlivens his re-perusal of things past when, as an old man, he returns to "the house/ Of my own life":

> There all the doors stand open
> Perpetually, and the rooms ring with sweet voices,
> And there my long life's seasons sound their changes,
> Childhood and youth and manhood all together,
> And welcome waits, and not a room but is
> My own, beloved and longed for.
>
> ("The Return")

Reading his poems, I meet myself as I used to be, and things a small boy cared for, now vanished,

> The horses on the roundabout
> Still flying round the glittering ring
> That rusted fifty years ago.
> ("Into Thirty Centuries Born")

A hiatus opened in Muir's life between his idyllic childhood and the later years, at least partly fulfilled. The sandy waste between is painful to contemplate and might have been the most of it. But in his mature time, the years of childhood returned from beyond oblivion, and they gave him what he called "a symbolical stage on which the drama of human life can play itself out." This stage was Orkney, a group of islands off the north coast of Scotland where he was born in 1887. Without his knowing it, he said, the bare landscape became "a universal landscape." Strange blessings never in Paradise fell from its beclouded skies.

"Symbolical" sends up the wrong signals, however, tempting us to look for occulted meanings under the surface. But Muir's poetry is superficial, true on both sides of his figures of speech. Partly the myth he celebrates is itself, that is, a fiction:

> My childhood all a myth
> Enacted in a distant isle;
> Time with his hourglass and his scythe
> Stood dreaming on the dial,
> And did not move the whole day long
> That immobility might save
> Continually the dying song,
> The flower, the falling wave.
> And at each corner of the wood
> In which I played the ancient play,
> Guarding the traditional day
> The faithful watchers stood.
> ("The Myth")

This vision of immobility differs from the fantasies all of us cherish in that it is ambiguous, hence more nearly true.

"Ambiguous" doesn't mean murky. For Muir it means that his vision is believable, also a chimera, not one or the other but both at once. Shakespeare in *The Winter's Tale* offers an analogue. "When you do dance," says the play's young hero, addressing his beloved,

> I wish you
> A wave o' the' sea, that you might ever do
> Nothing but that—move still, still so,
> And own no other function.

The wish is hardly mocked, and in fact the play entertains it, part of its enormous appeal. Inevitably, though, the wave breaks, and we see that perfect stasis, like enduring childhood, is "all a myth." Though Muir's yearned-for place is back there in time, like Orkney, the present day with its sad insufficiencies is just over the wall or scaling the wall. The poetry depends for its success on this close relation.

The title poem of Muir's last volume locates him:

> One foot in Eden still, I stand
> And look across the other land.

His vantage point matters, not least for comparison, but it's the other land that gives the poetry its bite:

> What had Eden ever to say
> Of hope and faith and pity and love
> Until was buried all its day?

Another near-perfect poem, "In Love for Long," takes substance from the "crying sorrows" that besiege it, and the love it evokes, "in wrong, beyond wrong," is realized as it acknowledges constraint.

> This love a moment known
> For what I do not know
> And in a moment gone
> Is like the happy doe
> That keeps its perfect laws
> Between the tiger's paws
> And vindicates its cause.

Particular things grow in Muir's Eden, not etiolated either like Milton's in the Eden of *Paradise Lost* but telling of the earth they grew in. A function of their particularity is that they are subject to time. The poet saw them first at a range of two or three feet. (Children are the original New Critics, eyes right down on the subject.) "A carnival of birth and death," his farm on Orkney featured copulation and killing. But those are only abstractions until the word is made flesh. In the *Autobiography*, this happens. His father leads out the bull to serve the cow; a neighbor sticks the pig. Down the road horses are coming and he can hear them. Their hooves drum in the poetry, beginning with the first book of 1925. One of the permanent poems is called "The Horses."

In an uncollected poem, "There's Nothing Here," Muir's roughneck cousin Sutherland is before us. Clay clings to his body as he takes the plough stilts in hand. He smells of peat, dung, and cattle, and the taste of the dram is still in his mouth. Waking up after death, he finds himself in heaven, where not even a shadow falls. How can he live without substance and shadow?

Muir's kind of seeing doesn't ascend to conceptual truth, and the thing seen isn't strained of impurities. This defines but obviously delimits its nature. No extrapolations in his poetry. His religious side would like it otherwise but he doesn't indulge it, too scrupulous a poet for that. A carnal self apprehends what he looks at, laying on it rough hands, the way our prehensile thumb apprehends or takes hold of. Mnemonic tetrameters, easy to remember but not easy to parse, give the gist of what we learn in his Eden:

> Men are made of what is made,
> The meat, the drink, the life, the corn,
> Laid up by them, in them reborn.
> ("The Island")

Being thick with substance, the life these lines register comes home to us powerfully, and has only a limited term.

"Moses," a poem about the prophet, not a far-seeing one, comments on this paradox. Though he is granted the Pisgah-sight, he doesn't raise his eyes much, satisfied with "byre, barn and stall" in the foreground. Embodied things, they don't translate, nor can they travel "beyond the shore of space." On the shore you see girl and angel in the Fra Angelico painting ("The Annunciation"). From their meeting comes the incarnate God, uniquely the gift of Christianity, not in the giving of the Logos.

Of course the gift is qualified, and what you can apprehend will finally slip through your fingers. That is why Muir commits to Plato. His "is the truest poetry," he said (in a late poem, "I Have Been Taught"), willing us to think of the shadows on the cave wall. Noumenal things, not there to the eye, cast these shadows. Muir wanted to possess the noumena, craving the cause of the effect. This desire, an ancient one, is probably illicit, given what we are, purblind creatures who lack the ability to see into things or see them all round. But Muir, aware that our view can only be a purview, never left off his passion for the world of abstractions.

The passion is in the poetry, bitten with the impulse to brush aside thronging shadows and come to the true. Perhaps it fortifies the poetry, as when strong liquor mixes with wine. The shadows detain him, however, bringing "rare felicities." In one poem, "Double Absence," "A sycamore/ Holds on its topmost tip a singing thrush," turning its breast toward the sun. The thrush is only its phenomenal self and points to nothing beyond, but he sees it and lends us his eyes.

\*    \*    \*

Muir's success is partial, and there are things he can't do. He doesn't range widely, he keeps his voice down (no organ music, etc.), and what he says is lightly inflected. This lowers his stature but gains for him too, and having trained you to hear him, he needn't shout from the rooftops. Intentionality, as it might be a dominie's, is part of his makeup. When he gives it room, the poem is pulled earthwards. But natural piety muffles the didactic impulse, and much of the poetry seems to have no purpose but itself.

The first of two poems called "Dialogue" shows these opposing strains working against each other. On an evening when all is still,

> the bird in flight hangs tranced upon the air,
> Flying and yet at rest, as if time's work were over,
> And the sun burns red and still on the bole of the yew-
>     tree,
> And the workman, his day ended, stands and listens,
> Thinking of home....

In poetry like this, almost Imagist in its feeling and limited scope, the workman needn't think of anything, and perhaps his thought is felt as intrusive.

Meanwhile, poets for whom intention is the sine qua non are enforcing conclusions. Muir has his affinities with these purposeful poets, sometimes treating description as a *point d'appui*. This is the approved modern method, illustrated, for example, in the novel as perfected by James. In vogue until the other day, it wants every detail to serve the overarching idea. The passage quoted from "Dialogue" moves towards this idea, ostensibly the center where the poem's energy collects or ought to. More than bird, sun, tree, and workman, Muir's recurring question is supposed to govern. His dead kinsmen say what it is:

> Long since we lost a road,
> And feel the ghost of an ethereal sorrow
> Passing, and lighting or darkening all the house....
> Does that road still run somewhere in the world?

The question is held back until the climax, making it appear the poem's important business. But readers who listen to the poem rather than the poet on his official side will take it as an epicenter, not the true center. The energy that thrills us pulses in the surround. Official Muir is deferring to his bent for abstraction, but the poem that engages us goes the other way. You could say that despite him, the adverb counts more than the noun.

The régisseurial temperament, in the saddle for a long time, honors different priorities. "Off the point" is a term of reproach. Some poems of Wordsworth's, like this one of Muir's, find the bias of the régisseur uncongenial. In "The Ruined Cottage," the heroine who lives there, though she is a figure of much social import, is less important to the poet than the cold bare wall tricked with weeds and spear grass. The mixing up of real and ostensible purpose doesn't embarrass poetry like Wordsworth's and Muir's. Both do best when they lower their eyes. Inevitably, they leave the Pisgah-sight to others.

Generally a single qualifier goes with Muir's substantives, or the noun stands alone: "grass in the rain,/ Light on the land, sun on the sea," etc. ("The Child Dying"). His flat enumerative style in poems like "The Good Town": "mounds of rubble... shattered piers, half-windows, broken arches.... gaping bridges... the quiet river... the small green hills," comes as close to ground level as poetry can get without losing its charter. He courted losing it. Poetry was "all that fiddle," and he wanted to cut to the chase.

He lacked the manage of a great rhetoric like Yeats's, the price an honest man pays for his horror of rodomontade. Yeats, he said, drew his rhetorical power from the people, who "gave him the liberty to speak of anything, while obliging him to speak of certain things" (*The Estate of Poetry*). Why this should be true of rough rugheaded kerns in Ireland but not of grave livers in Scotland is beyond me, and I think "fit audience, though few" is the best any writer in our time can hope for.

Muir thought otherwise, hoping to recover the long-vanished audience that had the Border Ballads on the tip of its tongue. His own work, said Archibald MacLeish, partly justifies his hope that "a great theme greatly treated might still put poetry back in its old place." The great theme is Scotland Betrayed, a version of the Fall in the Garden. Poems that develop it are "Scotland's Winter," "The Difficult Land," "Complaint of the Dying Peasantry," "The Refugees Born for a Land Unknown," "Scotland 1941." In matters of moment like this one, however, stunning reversals only cheapen. Scotland's great days, devolution notwithstanding, are gone with the wind, and poetry's once ample audience has gone with them.

Going on half a century after his death, Muir's *Collected Poems* are out of print in America. He himself isn't widely remembered. Who is, though? "California!" someone said, when I brought up his name. "The naturalist?" But the audience that doesn't read him is poorer for that. Its electronic culture offers no substitute for his mix of Christian Platonism plus a countryman's more corporeal reading. Fusing in poems like "Thought and Image," his ill-assorted materials make a solid join. (It's the unlikely pair that sticks together.)

Naked thought is abstract and therefore unconvincing, like King Lear's "unaccommodated man." Muir understood this. In so many words, he said that thought must find an image to ratify its truth. Like Donne's great prince in "The Ecstasy," it lies in prison until it can descend "to affections and to faculties." En route to its incarnation, the thought grows intimate with beast and herb and stone, mating at last with dull earth. In that way the miracle happens, and "a Child in body bound" is born among the cattle in a byre. Time passes until, braced by wood and iron, he dies engrafted on a tree.

> All that had waited for his birth
> Were round him then in dusty night,

not only the souls and angels but beasts, insects, plants, and the elements that make up the world.

The Platonic psychology is fanciful, even fantastic. An image for it is the wild arabesques Celtic artisans worked into their silver and bronze ware. But a geometer's eye reined in their extravagance, and Muir's provincial side does this for his thought. Without the leavening of the common tongue and common sensibility, the impalpable thought, running free, would dissipate in thin air.

Muir's best, like everyone else's, is imperfect. Necessarily constrained, he saw the world through a glass darkly. This medium or window includes diction, figurative language, and poetic form. The yield for him was more than clamping down or reining in, though. Paradoxically, liberation went with constraint.

For the truth is that our privations redeem us. The sonnet form to which Muir sometimes submitted is one of them. Another is the abbreviated line, his habitual constraint. Hard to think of the poetry without this yoke he bowed his neck to. "Give," he tells a loved woman, "but have something still to give." When every barrier falls, we are nothing. An ancient scorner said to him once,

> Beware
> The road that has no corner
> Where you can linger and stare.
> Choose the square.
> ("Circle and Square")

John Buchan, a Scot who overlapped him in time, gives Muir's likeness. In his autobiography, Buchan says of himself that he was born "with the same temperament as the Platonists of the early seventeenth century." Compromised men with a foot in either camp, they "combined a passion for the unseen and the eternal with a delight in the seen and the temporal." Muir's poetry makes this dichotomy vivid. Looking beyond the sight line, it hopes for a glimpse of the noumenal world. But poems like "The Last War" announce a double allegiance, and I make them characteristic. In love with the unseen, they take strength from the physical world and the art that shapes it: "all that is full-grown/ In nature, and all that is with hands well-made."

# 7

## George Mackay Brown and the Orkney Islands

Before his death in 1996, George Mackay Brown published more than thirty volumes of poems, plays, novels, short stories, and essays. The place he lived and died in is his single subject, and one of his titles, *An Orkney Tapestry*, stands for all the others. In a cosmopolitan age, he was certainly provincial. But memorizing Orkney kept him on the qui vive. I once knew a man who had only one book, *Moby Dick*. He reread it every year and said it still surprised him.

Orkney, an archipelago-size cluster of islands, lies off the northeast coast of Scotland. Between it and John o' Groats, the Atlantic and the North Sea shoulder each other, and sometimes island weather is all wildness and wet. But people have lived there for more than 5,000 years, and upwards of 19,000 still do. Many, craving the babble of the modern world, have pulled up stakes, however, leaving a ghostly landscape behind. Brown's sense of Orkney reflects this:

> Vacant now,
> It waits, an overturned grain jar,
> Abandoned in the world's flight from poverty, silence,
>     sanctity.

Two impressive poets of the twentieth century are "Orcadians." The better known one, Edwin Muir, ranged deep in the racial memory. At home in other lands, he was a good European. Brown, more restricted in life and art, looks like a minor poet beside him.

The appearance is beguiling, though. Orkney's sea and earth, creel and plough, fish and cornstalk, shore people and shepherds (all these pairings are his) compose the warp and weft of his poems. No material for poetry is more prosperous. Brown isn't a topical poet, and has nothing to say of the oil and uranium deposits in and around the islands, much talked about in the press. In calling him minor, I don't intend a derogation. John Clare is a minor poet, Alfred Sisley a minor painter, Henry Lawes is a minor composer, and this is the company he keeps.

His compass is narrow—"I rent and till a patch of dirt/ Not much bigger than my coat," he says (in "Eynhallow")--but partly the narrowness works for him. "Much riches in a little room" is a phrase for his poetry, suggesting its quality, also its limitation. He isn't a miniaturist, however, but a sure-handed mason, "master of the granite hewing, squaring, last/ pure chiseling" ("Foresterhill"). In a seven-part poem on the death of St. Magnus, his poetic line is "like old carved stones." Simplicity like his comes from racking your brains, though the labor mustn't be noticed. A short-lines poem, "Lighting Candles in Midwinter," invokes the saint of our shortest day:

> Sweet St. Lucy be kind
> To us poor and wintered and blind—

but though scope is abridged and the direction centripetal, the descriptive terms take in a lot of ground.

Born into a world of silence "broken acceptably by wind and sea," Brown grew old in a world where silence is the one unendurable thing, and the radio, etc., clicks on at first light. In a prose meditation, "Magi," he dreams back to his Orkney childhood when he "owned the whole world, corn and buttercup and rockpool, and the men and women and animals put looks of love on me and on each other." But the idyllic place has its dark underside, accommodating the heart's desperate wickedness. If the tone of that is too moral, say that Brown's Eden makes room for man's long love affair with violence. Much of Scotland's bloody history, culminating in the defeat at Culloden, is in these lines from "The Escape of the Hart":

> Cold it was in the corrie that morning,
> A harsh rain. We drew the prince

Round by the eyrie, the thunders of new water.
The Saxons lay in the next glen.
We signed our bread with holy crosses. Then,
Red on the moon, through shrouds and prisms of fog,
            we saw the hunters
Issue like beads of blood.

Born in Stromness on Orkney's largest island in 1921, he died there seventy-five years later. Stromness, a modern town, dates from the sixteenth century, and one of his longer poems remembers its founders, a married couple, innkeepers, who couldn't know what the future held:

Tall houses hewn from granite,
Piers on the tidal mark,
Yawl and cobble-noust gathered,
    William and Mareon Clark.

The town comes down to the water, and as you sail into the harbor the shoreline, "a ballad in stone," surprises your senses. Landward, the houses are built into a steep granite-studded hill; seaward, they sit on stone piers in the Hamnavoe, an arm of the sea. The composition they make, blue rectangles and vertical cubes, cancels out all but the idea of buildings, nearly resolving to geometric form. Late paintings by Cezanne are like this.

Blue slate, elsewhere a rich man's roofing but in Orkney more common than shingling, gives houses in the islands their air of the abstract. Brown's poetry is like this, not abstract meaning tenuous but pared down almost to outline. Where the Orkney sun strikes against the roofs in Stromness, the slate shows as hard-edged planes that leave half their surface in shadow. The land isn't hard, though, nor sharply demarcated, but a checkerboard of green and greenish-yellow fields flowing into each other. Cattle, both beef and dairy, crop the fields, and the sulfur-yellow color is rape seed, the source of canola. Beyond the water, always there on the periphery, rise the hills of another island, covered by heather in season. Wind, omnipresent too, ripples the green grass, and thistles brighten the stone walls that run with the roads. The thistle, its jagged prickliness redeemed by the purplish-red flower, is Scotland's emblem. It looks at home in Orkney.

Near land's end a gray stone church, boarded up and closed to worshipers, stands beside a stone-walled cemetery, long since disused. Brown has a reminiscence of a church or chapel like it, "between Cornfield and Shore" out of Stromness:

> Above that ebb that gray uprooted wall
> Was arch and chancel, choir and sanctuary,
> A solid round of stone and ritual.
> Knox brought all down in his wild hogmanay.

Knox is John Knox, the sixteenth-century preacher who railed against cakes and ale, and Hogmanay is New Year's Eve in Scotland, ironically a time for revels.

But the image of an ampler time, superseded by the modern world, isn't altogether accurate. When you take the steamer out of Stromness, if your voyage is the longer one around the coast to Aberdeen, little boys in full-kilted uniform give you a sendoff at dockside. They belong to the Stromness Pipe Band, specializing in favorites of the Jacobite risings, "Will Ye No Come Back Again" and "The Bonnets of Bonnie Dundee." Elsewhere perhaps the "auld sangs" are dying, but in Orkney they still quicken the blood. The young still submit to the discipline of the bagpipes. Privation in this northern land seems a way to fulfillment, a lesson not lost on Brown.

He lived much in Orkney (as when we say that Shakespeare lived much in the mind), taking brief excursions outside. One was to New Battle Abbey in Dalkeith, an adult education college reopened after World War II with Edwin Muir as warden. Brown was just into his thirties when he got this chance to lick his natural self in shape. He writes about the experience in his autobiography, a modern classic (*For the Islands I Sing*, 1997). Between him and the schoolmaster's temperament a gulf opens, however. Like Christ in his poem on "The Stations of the Cross," he "clung close to the curve of the world." Though he wasn't anti-intellect, he wasn't open-minded either, our time's desideratum but a plaguey thing to be, and his poems are inflected and circumscribed by his own value system and his personal reading of history. Going back a thousand years to the legends gathered in the *Orkneyinga Saga*, they come up to his father and stop there.

In "Hamnavoe," reenacting a day beside the sheltered harbor, he thought of his father's "gay poverty" that kept a son's innocence from the black wind:

> And because, under equality's sun,
> All things wear now to a common soiling,
>   In the fire of images
>   Gladly I put my hand
>   To save that day for him.

The father, schooled by the public library, brought home the books that nourished the son. To hear him and others tell it, the islands and Highlands were auspicious for poetry. All Scots poetry is sad—never mind the capering that goes on at Burns Nicht, when Scots around the world celebrate the birthday of their national poet. In Brown's poem for Culloden, the woman at her loom sings "the beauty of defeat." He knew about defeat in his bones.

But not "alienation." His people were of the Highlands and he kept the good old way. In the century before his birth, Highlanders endured the Clearances, driven from their crofts in the valleys, their roofs burned over their heads. His Scots mother, born across the Pentland Firth, spoke only Gaelic until she went to school, where the masters, men of the Ascendancy class, sought to make it an embarrassment. Brown might have grown up a firebrand, like Hugh MacDiarmid, but knew that most protest is puerile. MacDiarmid, in his best poems, knew this too.

Brown's father, a tailor and occasional postman, felt deeply for the urban poor. He read Robert Tressell's *Ragged Trousered Philanthropists*, that preposterous but moving novel in which the villain gets his at last, "catching" cancer from the clothing he's stolen off the dying hero. The father would have called himself a socialist, except that Marx's chilly sociology repelled him. His model leader was Keir Hardie, a British version of Eugene Victor Debs. For both of them, great men, socialism was a cry of pain.

The pain isn't likely to go away. Contractual solutions, though offered as a cure-all, don't deal with the ills flesh is heir to, and Brown understood this. "Deep in the hold/ The jars of love we bore," says an occasional poem of his ("for a 25th Wedding Anniversary").

> All who trade in that freightage
> Dread the devourings of time, and salt, and tare.

Seeing what's coming, this poet doesn't flinch, though. The cover of his *Selected Poems* (1996), available in America from the University of Iowa Press, shows what he looked like, jut jaw, thrust-out underlip, a prow of a nose, cold eyes under frown lines, thick untidy gray hair. A tough hatchet face, it doesn't ask quarter and gives none.

*    *    *

You can rent a car in Orkney but everything is so near, the cattle behind fences only an arm's length away, the little corn-patched hills like the quilt they cover your bed with, that pedaling a bike seems to suit decorum better. The automobile leaves its telltale, however. Gas pumps, no disguising them, poke up from the ground, and here and there cast-off tires or a rusting chassis stare you down. The scattering of twentieth-century junk turns the rural landscape squalid, but the overlay is just that, only "paste and cover" to the bones underneath. Fill a few dumpsters with this Johnny-come-lately trash and you are back in the beginning, Orkney as it used to be. This is Brown's metier, laying bare the foundation.

Scara Brae, due north of Stromness, puts ancient Orkney before you. Brown gives its color in his poem "Vinland":

> Salt in the mouth,
> The rage
> Of north wind at morning,
> Sodden crust,
> Cold kissings of rain.

A network of huts built from unmortared stone, this Stone Age survival lay entombed for forty centuries under sand dunes by the seashore until time scoured them off. Before the Pyramids and the Great Wall of China, people were living at Scara Brae. They slept in stone bunk beds, stored their clothing in stone dressers and their utensils in cupboards hollowed out from the rock. Though they had fireplaces, being cold must have been their normal condition. The damp gave them arthritis. Their stone beds seem very small.

Beyond Scara Brae is the Brough of Birsay, a tidal islet facing the ocean and only accessible, like Mt. St. Michel, at low water. On this islet a great medieval earl built a palace with central heating, also the church he was buried in, two years before the Norman Conquest of England. The church lived in Brown's memory: three arches on the green holm, a nearby village reachable at ebb tide ("Horseman and Seals, Birsay"). Rotting seaweed wrinkles your nostrils as you walk the Brough of Birsay. Sky, dwarfing the land, is slate gray, shot with patches of pearly white, color by Tiepolo. Inland from the Brough a later earl built another castle, still imposing today. Red-haired Scottish boys and girls are playing in the remains of its tower.

As you cycle east out of Stromness, the stone dwellings by the road are modern but darkened with the immemorial rain. Gray stucco, called "rendering," covers many of them, and twin chimney pots stick up from the tops of chimneys like cows' teats. Rose of Sharon grows in front gardens, and by the wayside a red flower with a yellow button, primula scotica. Below the hills that rim the fields, bales of hay lean together like stacked rifles.

Mixing new and old is the convention in Orkney, and the "henge" monuments (like Stonehenge) of Stenness and Brodgar are silhouetted against the sky as they have been for millennia. Brown in his Brodgar Poems makes the huge stones speak. They evoke the Titans, old gods thrust under ground by the new dispensation but striving to break free of their confinement. Farmers over the centuries have quarried them for their houses and barns, but at Brodgar twenty-seven stones still look out to sea, nine more lying toppled around them. Both henges occupy the skinny neck of land that separates the saltwater Loch of Stenness from the freshwater Loch of Harray. Salt kills, and this sliver of land is our "moat defensive," keeping destruction at bay. Swans float on the water and fishing skiffs are pulled up on the foreshore. The whiff of ancient sacrifice hangs about the uncanny place. Historians say that raising its stones took as many as 200,000 man-hours, labor of Neolithic times, five thousand years ago.

A circle having neither beginning nor end, the ring of standing stones spoke to Brown's imagination. "The birds return," he said, "The waters rise,"

> Come, dancer, go
> Step by circle
> The reel endures.
> ("Old Man")

A loosely knit series, Brown's Brodgar Poems follow the procession, youth leading off, age on its heels. "She who threw marigolds over you" becomes a crone with cindery breath, then the round of life begins again. Looking ahead to our new millenium, Brown saw how moderns, though differing in their means to the end from the stone-breakers and horizon-breakers of 3000 B.C., don't differ in last things. "Whiggish" people in our time, supposing that the course of things is always upward, won't believe this.

A little to the northeast, in the burial cairn at Maeshowe, a circular ditch encloses the tomb and a circle describes the lives of the men and women who lay there. To reach the burial chamber you have to bend over, almost getting down on all fours. That is how we manage when starting out in life, and some end up like that too. The people buried at Maeshowe lived on the average twenty to twenty-five years but were physically like us, subject to the same wear and tear. Brown, making connections, says "We all go under the hill."

A thousand years ago Viking marauders, returning from a crusade to the Holy Land, broke open the tomb at Maeshowe. With an ax brought from Iceland, they carved runic writing into the walls, wanting to be remembered. Like the people of Orkney they perished in turn, maybe in some sword fight "About some royal mixup or other." For one of them, dead under a horse's hoof, Brown wrote an epitaph:

> I said, 'Farewell, Rolf,
> It goes well with you, friend.
> Flesh-unfastened.

This doesn't waste words but death comes to all, and decorum won't permit much enlarging.

Death, Brown's familiar, brings out a laconic and stoical poet. His Seven Ages of Man "didn't take long to tell" ("Countryman"), less than Shakespeare's. He thinks interrogating silence is the poet's true task, and in "Hill Runes," a good generic title for the poetry, including in it the sense of gnomic, he interrogates "the clay book," furrow by furrow. He isn't a discursive poet, however, and the result is less answers than inscriptions:

Early on Monday last
There came a wave and stood above your mast.
("The Death of Peter Esson")

What is man?
A head bent over fish and bread and ale.
Outside, the long furrow.
Through a door, a board with a shape on it.
("Our Lady of the Waves")

Bright door, black door,
Beak-and-wing hurtling through.
("Bird in the Lighted Hall")

This last seems to remember the Old English writer Bede, not an influence, a like sensibility. For Brown, twelve hundred years later, life is a bird flying briefly into light and out again into darkness.

But Brown is alive to that "one touch of nature" without which no art has much meaning. His version of life is more than its outline in this image of a bridegroom,

Standing
With a bright shivering ring
Beside that tall whiteness
In the hushed barn
Tonight
When the minister urges the gold circlet
from fingers to finger.
("Seal Island Anthology, 1875")

What the man and woman in the poem are doing is formal, though not perfunctory, and the ceremony is hardly peculiar to either. Even so, how it takes him and us!

Orkney's countryside, not much differentiated, mirrors the poem and predicts it. Black cattle like dots on snowy paper move across the fields, their sameness relieved only by a bright rectangle of rape seed. West of Kirkwall, however, a windbreak of trees does its best to defend a farmstead, incidentally breaking the monotony of the skyline. Brown's poetry shares something with this windbreak, and I think we say that in nature as for poetry, value isn't exhausted in function.

A "homily" (his title) tells of childhood when there is only the garden, no gate or road beyond it. Then in youth comes a call in the night, and we go out under the stars. As age begins, the call still delights us, but

> The sun sets on our laboring urgency.
> We hurry to find an inn
> With fire and bottle, fish and bread.
> It thickens to black snow.
> Breath, heart are snagged with nets of blizzard.

Loneliness is all, "no fellow pilgrims on that road." But what happens in the garden, under the stars, or in the inn at journey's end, though off the point for a paradigm, makes a difference.

In Brown's memory of Orkney, the starkest fact is the death of St. Magnus, murdered on Easter Monday in 1117. The saint is buried in the cathedral in Kirkwall, Orkney's largest town, and if you keep going to the other side of the island you reach it. St. Magnus cathedral, though outsize for the smallish place it ministers to, is of the earth earthy, keeping proportion. Red sandstone, like clay, assimilates it to the land. The form of its rounded arches is like the bowl of the sky, and its immense pillars are like trees in the forest. To the perpendicular style of gothic we are grateful for many things, not least audacity, but the repose of this Romanesque church isn't one.

The ruined palaces across the road seem imagined by a poet, not a mordant poet, though their story is mordant, only unillusioned. In the great hall of the Earl's Palace, the last earl of Orkney held court until the king in Edinburgh caught him and chopped off his head. An embittered king of Norway died in the Bishop's Palace eight hundred years ago, nursing his defeat at Largs on the west coast of Scotland. Coming under cover of darkness, he had thought to take the Scots by surprise but his men trod on the thistle, and their yelping set off the alarm.

Brown remembers Largs, where his Viking warriors are sailing with a thousand swords, "tomorrow." Death in their annals is always just around the corner, and that is the value to poetry of Orkney's heroic past. Cinching the narrative whose termini are birth and death, in that way getting rid of the indifferent clutter between them, it makes our common lot all the clearer.

Earl Hakon murdered St. Magnus, and incredibly—except that history has many examples like it—he ranks among the greatest of the Orkney earls. "So shines a good deed in a naughty world." Brown's comment (from *The Merchant of Venice*) is certainly ironic and possibly hopeful. The Christian story engages him often, the Nativity part of it touching him most. The stones of the desert town "flush" when Christ is born ("The Lodging"); a new star tells the Wisemen that "The time is come/ For exile" ("The Golden Door: Three Kings"). Brown mines the birth in the manger for its connections to poverty and the silence that comes with winter. Together, they breed sanctity.

I don't know that he would claim more than that. In Orkney men were bloody-minded, and whether Christianity changed them, or changed anything, he doesn't say. It left a perfume, however. In my choice for his best lines (from "A Child's Calendar"), he invokes the Savior:

> Some December midnight
> Christ, lord, lie warm in our byre.
> Here are stars, an ox, poverty enough.

During the Second World War, Italian prisoners, captured in the African desert, built a chapel on Orkney, and all who visit it must marvel at the craft that made something from nothing. Defeated and far from home, the men of Camp 60 wouldn't let the spirit sink into torpor. The triangular facade of their church is ridged with fleur-de-lis and topped with a Christian Cross like a sunburst. Molded from cement, the crucified Christ hangs on a barbed-wire framework. Over the wartime Nissen huts that give the church a skin, the barrel-vault ceiling looks real.

But the Madonna on the apse above the altar, modeled on one of sentimental Murillo's, sheds a warmth like neon over Brown's winter landscape. Throw the switch and the warmth is gone. Religiosity, sounding like religion but a universe apart, doesn't console the poet. On his reading all are fated, not in the stagy sense scripted by Thomas Hardy, fated by nature. Like Orkney's Earl Patrick, who may or may not have been Christian,

> Every man drinks his own cup of death.
> Whatever road he takes, forest or firth

Or mountain path or moor scratchy with whins,
At the end of the road is the cup brimming with shadows.
                                            ("The Killers")

Life resolves to a few modest images, lifting lobsters from the
sea, a girl at a rockpool shaking out yellow hair. Brown isn't dour
and this vision has its charm. The reward of our labors in the after-
life doesn't seem much, though, "a quieter alehouse,/ Free drink,
no hangovers." ("Orkneymen at Clontarf, AD 1014) They drink
hard in Heaven, picking up where they left off on earth.

Southwest of Kirkwall the Earl's "Bu" honored John Barleycorn,
after whom a ballad of Brown's is named. Next to the Bu is a ruined
Christian church, "cheek by jowl" as they used to say, suggesting
the intimate relation between them. Ready for broaching, large casks
of ale were stored in the Bu, incitements to violence, sometimes
savage death. Breaking off their bloody drinking bouts, men who
wanted to pray "went down steps from the hall to the church," according to the Orkneyinga Saga. Earl Hakon, he who murdered St.
Magnus, built the church, copied from the Church of the Holy Sep-
ulcher in Jerusalem. Like a conscience-stricken hero in Shakespeare
who intends a voyage to the Holy Land, he meant it to expiate his
crime.

From the little church at Orphir and its close-bosom friend the
Bu, the road to Kirkwall skirts the naval base at Scapa Flow. Before
Italians built the causeways, closing off access to the vessels riding
at anchor, a German sub sneaked in and out again, sending the
battleship *Royal Oak* to the bottom with a loss of over 800 men.
Earl Hakon's church, mute witness to many disasters, witnessed
this one. Its apse is still standing, a gray half-circle flecked with
white darkening to orange. The effect looks intentional, "like bright
metal on a sullen ground." But mortising the local stone they used
a mixture heavy on lime, giving the church its unusual color.

# 8

# My Two Masters

After Richard Blackmur died in 1965 and I moved from Princeton to Nashville, I got to know Allen Tate. That is only matter of fact. Much of the matter of every day in the lives of Tate and Blackmur is like it, and on one side they are like everybody else. The quiddity of Tate and Blackmur is something different, however, and offers reasons to remember them. At their highest pitch, they define the critical function. They do this from the side of artistic experience, testing the illusions our frailty inclines us to honor. This scrupulous testing is rare. Yeats says, in his poem for Major Robert Gregory, how we want the new friend to cherish the old. Among poems of his century, this was the one Allen put first. He didn't cherish the memory of his old friend Blackmur, however. There had been some causus belli between them, I didn't know what. I think it came down to the distrust of one superb presence for another. Superb as in "superbia," neither of them lacking for pride. My two masters were patient of pretension in themselves, jealous of it in anybody else. They confronted the world as from peaks on Mt. Rushmore. That was comic and diminishing. But each had his impersonal side.

Allen Tate was born in Winchester, Kentucky, November 19, 1899, R. P. Blackmur in Springfield, Massachusetts, January 25, 1904. The few years that separate them make an important difference. In unexpected ways the provenance does too. Blackmur, from the urban and industrial North, is the type of the indigenous man; Tate the Southern Agrarian is the type of the cosmopolitan. The criticism and poetry each of them wrote declare this identity. Tate missed the First World War by a matter of months. Later he went to New York City to live and then he lived in Paris. Altogether he is a

101

man of the generation of Kenneth Burke and Malcolm Cowley, for whom the war and its aftermath were decisive. He imagined himself a provincial but was equally at home on both sides of the Atlantic and both sides of Mason-Dixon. Blackmur's first encounter with Europe waited on his middle age, and the Dome and the Rotonde were a closed book to him. He knew the Lost Generation only through books. "I think he got to Havana once," said his early friend Lincoln Kirstein, meaning this for a sneer. In America he didn't travel much, unless the need to make money sent him on the lecture circuit. He was a stay-at-home, and he divided his life between New England—by preference Washington County way Down East—and Princeton, New Jersey, than which no community is more insular or sufficient to itself.

Tate entered Vanderbilt in 1918 from "a rural-smalltown society that had only a superficial Victorian veneer pasted over what was still an eighteenth-century way of living." He liked to say that Kentucky had seceded from the Union in 1865. As far as he knew, it hadn't gone back in. This notion fostered contentiousness in Allen, who carried his apartness like a flag. When Blackmur was an infant, his parents moved from Springfield to New York City, then to Cambridge. He grew up in a boardinghouse near the Harvard Yard. His boyhood years hadn't much to commend them, and when he got older he hid them from view. If he stood apart that was only as the urban poor, having no option, stand apart. As Yeats said of Keats, "I see a schoolboy when I think of him,/ With face and nose pressed to a sweet-shop window." The letters he wrote in his teens define the city-bred person. He never pulled a flower until he was into his twenties. Tate as a boy grew up in bluegrass country, and later he made a cult of the land. He liked to fish, he liked to swim, and his best poem shows him with water on the brain. You get the sense that all his life he looked back to the good time in the beginning. But like the moneylender in Horace's "Beatus ille" poem, he cared for the bucolic life only by turns.

In his middle years Tate was briefly a librarian for the Library of Congress. Being in libraries made him unhappy, though. Maybe five hundred books sufficed for a long life. He poked fun at Thomas Wolfe, who said he had read twenty thousand. But the man who didn't like libraries was a book unto himself. His learning was prodigious, and unlike Blackmur he wasn't put to pretending. John

Crowe Ransom was his teacher and "taught us," Allen said, "Kantian aesthetics and a philosophical dualism, tinged with Christian theology, but ultimately derived from the Nichomachian ethics." That makes a mouthful. Blackmur also was learned, but his formal credentials weren't nearly so impressive. He never finished high school, and often in his writing you sense that he is mustering credentials and you sense the uncertainty of the self-taught man. He was ignorant of languages, though he tried hard to mend his ignorance through self-schooling. "His theories (if his ideas ever reach that level of logical abstraction) are perhaps too simple for our taste and too improvised; but his reading is disciplined and acute." That is Tate's version of Dr. Johnson, and it holds for Blackmur, too.

Conrad Aiken, a friend of Blackmur's from *Hound & Horn* days, called his reading myopic. He meant that Richard kept his eye too close to the page, so saw each word and even each syllable as distinct. On this myopia, if that is what it was, his New Critical writing depended. Though he failed to estimate the greatness of Robert Frost, in company with all his fellow New Critics, he was alone among them in finding occasion for praise. An early line of Frost's dinned in his ear, "The fact is the sweetest dream that labor knows," and like Frost he could have written it over his lintel. This wasn't always true but Blackmur the autodidact, who pulled himself up by his bootstraps, made it true. In his twenties he began to visit Maine with the painter Helen Dickson, and after they were married he lived summers in Maine for the next twenty years. He learned about labor and learned about the land, and this unambitious learning, remote from ideas, informed his close-up way of reading and seeing. He said he knew what Frost was talking about, where the allusion was to wild orchids that fall before the scythe. He had tried hard to raise these things himself. Sometimes Frost slipped—"everybody slips." He ascribed to his Morgan colt in the poem called "The Runaway" a noise like miniature thunder. But "a colt is not shod. Unshod horses do not make thunderous sounds, especially if they don't weigh above forty or fifty pounds." This kind of prosaic knowledge and piety before it set Blackmur apart from the world of the university.

\* \* \*

Blackmur at Princeton, to which he came in 1940, is the intruder in the dust. Professor X and colleagues accepted the intrusive presence, misconceiving what Blackmur really was. Knowing what they were, they knew what he should be. They thought him an intellectualizer and thought he lived in words. He lived by the word, which says something different, but he lacked the gift and taste for conceptual thought. Like the twelfth-century cleric John of Salisbury, a hero of his, he preferred doubting to defining. He was by temperament a medieval Catholic, in other words an agnostic. Neither had all the answers, saying characteristically, "I don't know."

The doubting habit inclined him to accept "ignorance as the humbled form of knowledge." He pursued knowledge in its divers shapes, including the trivial, "to the point where they add to ignorance" rather than confess it. Then, he thought, the best response was silence. This habit and this pursuit made affinities easy but allegiance impossible. His colleagues heard the silences. They had no inkling of the double agent who owed allegiance to no sect or class or theory and who rejected impartially the Marxism of Malcolm Cowley and the Christianity of T. S. Eliot, disbelieving that "any particular frame of faith, political, moral, or religious, can fit any large body of men at any one time, or even, what is more important, the abler minds among it."

Off and on at Princeton Blackmur kept a journal, and he recorded in it how "Tate came in and we talked more of our regular argument, he for hierarchy and absolute order, I for the disponible, non-Euclidean order." Disponible (unattached) is out of James, he of the sensibility so fine as never to have had it violated by an idea. The non-Euclidean order works the death of general statement. The order to which Blackmur appealed had its roots in particulars, so it kept shifting as the eye moved. You didn't go to Blackmur if you were looking for a rock on which to stand. Tate said that Blackmur's hallmark was "critical skepticism"; it made him a tentative critic. The life of the criticism is independent, by and large, of formal structures. That is what it means to be a formalist. Conceptual thought was for theologians, philosophers, classical scientists, and English professors who were shirking their job. Occam's razor was a very good razor to carry in your pocket and ought to be standard equipment for critics. *Entia non sunt multiplicanda praeter necessitatem.*

Don't multiply your concepts beyond necessity, Blackmur told the Japanese. Like a frog he didn't care much about the systematic organization of the way by which he jumped. Order, he said, taking order tactfully with his dogmatic colleague Yvor Winters, is only "the objective form of what you know."

If you look at Blackmur's criticism of the mid-thirties, you find it saluting, also exemplifying, the man of provisional temper. Shakespeare is admirable as he possessed "a mind full of many provisional faiths." Henry Adams, whose intelligence is "saltatory but serial," is "provisional in every position." The description speaks to Blackmur's own achievement. *Saltatory* and *provisional* are the binding terms. (*Saltatory*, a word he affected, is jumping, as in "saltimbocca," so good it jumps in your mouth.) Blackmur said he liked "to work by other people's prescription." This saying denotes the inspired opportunist. You give him a job to do, and in return he gives you value. It teased his mind, in his humility and pride, to work that way. Shakespeare worked that way.

*Provisional* means hospitable or catholic, also what holds only for this instant or this moment. Blackmur, like the Abbot Suger, another hero of the twelfth century, saw the moral universe not as a monochrome but as a spectrum of different colors which nonetheless make a harmony. He understood that the harmony might vanish tomorrow. His thought seems turbid partly because shallow clearness, the metier of Professor X, was unavailable to him. Often you feel uncertain in what direction the thought is flowing, "for even a contradiction was to him only a shade of difference, a complementary color." The New Critical Blackmur is not an exegete or moralist or historian of ideas. He is meditating at a remove—art's length—on the mingled yarn of our life.

Sometimes this meditating suffers from inanition, and Blackmur is satisfied to ad lib. That was always a favorite mode of discourse for him, and when it works it does wonders. But Blackmur, between the Numen and the Moha, has put on his singing robes, and the result is partly dust in the eyes. This is where Tate betters Blackmur and where the provincialism shows to disadvantage. Both gave their judgment on Emily Dickinson's poetry, and you don't have to prefer one to the other. But they do different things. Tate evokes the social context and brings it to bear. I don't mean that he is more nearly political than Blackmur, and I am merely fatigued when their supposed lack of political sophistication is urged against these New Critics. Both Tate and Blackmur found the place where literature and politics cross. (This is worth an essay in definition.) I mean that Tate's intelligence is better equipped for expository prose. Mostly he spurned the vaticinal mode, or you can say that it eluded him. Knowing how the context governs, he lets you see this, and he isn't surprised that after Emerson the literature of New England tastes like a sip of cambric tea. Blackmur is full of wild surmises, and sometimes astonished by what he has said.

Historical scholarship is indispensable, Allen Tate said, "pernicious only when some ham actor in an English department uses it to wring tears from the Sophomores, by describing the sad death of Percy Shelley." If you want to understand Donne and Eliot, you should begin early to read the classical languages and after that the philosophers. There is probably no other way. In an essay on Longinus and his critical treatise "On the Sublime" Tate corrected the historical scholars. The title they proposed looked like a solecism to him. Disclaiming the attempt to establish a correct title, he was on the way to doing this when he entered his disclaimer, and his Greek was up to what he was doing. An essay he wrote in the thirties begins: "The profession of letters in France dates, I believe, from the famous manifesto of Du Bellay and the Pléiade in 1549." The assured manner and the weight of information it carries are Tate's hallmark and his possession from the beginning. He was born to the manner.

Living on easy terms with the expensive furniture of his mind, he suffered sometimes from the belletristic disorder, too much port after dinner inducing intellectual gout. Sometimes he comes home as a very elegant academic critic, closer to the rest of us than he is to Blackmur. Everything he wrote is distinguished by clarity, but when he is merely clear his prose is quotidian. Blackmur's prose is tightfisted and not always clear but raises the level of discourse. The two of them on Ezra Pound illustrate this. Tate on Pound is intelligent and cordial: he inspirits us to read the way Edmund Wilson does. Unlike Blackmur, however, he never really closes with the poems. He intellectualizes, and issues are always on the horizon.

Blackmur, who lived in nice distinctions, distinguished between the intellectual and the intelligent or "apprehensive" man. He took laconic pride in his New England heritage. It put farmers and fishermen in his family tree. He wrote in one of his poems: "Once along this coast/ my fathers made their sail/ and were with all hands lost,/ outweathered in a gale." Tate thought the New England heritage spelled trouble. He isolated what he called "the heresy of New England" in the correspondence of Jefferson and John Adams, "where the two sages discuss the possibility of morals." Jefferson, he said, referred his judgment to taste. He relied on "custom, breeding, ingrained moral decision." Adams wasn't so lucky. He needed a "process of moral reasoning" that forced him to think out his role from abstract principle. In this distinction Tate discovered the superiority of the antebellum South. "The Southern mind was simple, not top-heavy with learning it had no need of, unintellectual and composed; it was personal and dramatic, rather than abstract and metaphysical; and it was sensuous because it lived close to a natural scene of great variety and interest." These formulations date from 1930 and give the character of Tate as perhaps he saw himself.

He wasn't like that at all. He was like the New England heretic he reprehends in the older Adams, self-consciously defining and fiercely reiterating his intellectual positions. "I have at times thought," wrote his friend Andrew Lytle (in *The Hero with the Private Parts*, 1966), "that he had advanced himself into tactically untenable positions, or used too much force upon what seemed only an outpost engagement." In defense of his positions, he displayed enormous intellectual flair, but sometimes his argumentative bias makes him comic. Sometimes, taking on the whole world, he is comic and poignant together, like Ransom's Captain Carpenter. The tragic Southerner, he said, had a religious life but no rational system to support it, no full-grown philosophy; so, when confronted with "the post-bellum temptations of the devil"—Tate means, as always, the rationalizing mind—he showed himself defenseless. This isn't, however, the character of Tate. It suggests the character of Blackmur the obdurate provincial, weak and strong in his provincialism.

Toward the end of his life, Allen said how "the typical Southern conversation is not going anywhere; it is not about anything." (This makes it resemble poetry.) Educated Northerners, on the other hand, "like their conversation to be about ideas." They are didactic and purposive. Tate in his criticism is didactic and purposive—he tells you this himself—and ideas constitute his fatal chimera. "The fallacy of communication in poetry" got his dander up, but he liked to inquire: "What does this mean?" and he liked to tell you. "Here I am a moralist," he wrote in 1936; and he asked his reader to remember that moralists are desperate persons who must "in their weaker moments squeeze a moral even out of modern poetry." Over the years he had a lot of weaker moments. Theories of education absorbed his attention. His subject was poetry, but other subjects kept asking for room. He talked about poetry, but in the midst of his talk he wanted to "bring to focus three attitudes of the modern world," etc. In 1945 he was "a little embarrassed at having used so many large conceptions, with so little specification." He got over his embarrassment, though.

Tate's many essays on generic subjects proclaim the atrabiliar man, inflamed by all that parti pris he disliked in Shelley and kept coming back to. "Large conceptions" ride him obsessively—the Negro, finance capitalism, the North, an abstract entity or dagger of the mind. He said how poetry "finds its true usefulness in its perfect inutility, a focus of repose for the will-driven intellect." This focus was the goal which beckoned for Tate, and sometimes he achieved it. But the man of letters wasn't just like the lilies of the field. He needed a "critical program" or he needed "dogma in criticism," and it was up to him to "propagate standards." Tate knew what they were, and he knew who had let down the bars. He named names. But he wrote whimsically of himself: "The demonology which attributes to a few persons the calamities of mankind is perhaps a necessary convention of economy in discourse." The self-conscious habit makes the difference. "In literature as in life," Allen said, "nothing reaches us pure." Not even the artist—maybe the artist least of all—can decide that experience must be either esthetic or practical. "It is never, as it comes to us, either/ or; it is always both/and."

Though Blackmur has his shrill obsessions, they are mostly "personal"—Hart Crane, D. H. Lawrence, E. E. Cummings (who lived down the street in Cambridge but whose family was better off). Characteristically he is the great neutral among critics, and sometimes he reads like intelligent litmus paper. He sees how poetry is kinetic, and he says it "moves along a line." But this doesn't describe how it soothes the savage breast. Poetry is kinetic as it confers importance on unimportant things. He thinks poetry aspires to a condition of tautology where things affect us only for themselves and only as they are themselves. This Blackmur stands in a direct line of descent from Oscar Wilde and the estheticians of the Mauve Decade. At his best and most hardhearted he takes you back to their master Ruskin, who wrote in the appendix to *Modern Painters*: "Does a man die at your feet, your business is not to help him but to note the colour of his lips."

Art is for art and butters no parsnips. Both Blackmur and Tate believed this, Tate believing other things too. "The seal of Princeton University," said Blackmur ironically, "is miraculously good in this respect"—i.e., what it says would be miraculous if true. "It says that if you will study hard, you will prosper under the numinous power of God." But prosperity doesn't turn on diligence, and the connection between poetry and progress or literature and morality is more willed than apparent. Blackmur didn't honor the connection. Like the myopic men in the poem by Robert Frost, he looked too near the earth, and his line of vision intersected its curve. Tate, writing to Kirstein, objected that Blackmur, for want of a "comprehensive view," took "a schoolmaster's delight in the small differences." That loses for him but is also his gain.

Tate, like his "cousin" Poe, spent his life hunting the comprehensive view, and his failure to harmonize different orders of experience shows in the failure to harmonize himself. In an essay on Poe he wrote how "when men find themselves cut off from reality they will frequently resort to magic rites to recover it." These magic rites are figured for him in his shibboleths and irrational dogmas. The least New Critical of the New Critics, paradoxically the most academic, he looked through reality, looking for a clue. In his perturbation he resembles John Donne, whom he called "one of the last Catholic allegorists." Like Donne, however—also like Blackmur—he escaped the petrifaction of dogma by throwing back insistently to lower-case things. He said aiming high was meaningless "unless the aim is sighted from a point below." Blackmur, said left-leaning friends like Alfred Kazin, aimed so low that he never saw the forest for the trees. In his dispassion, his myopic fixity, his want of ambition, he was Tate's despair—and a source of envy. "He looks like a horse of another color," Tate said in 1949, "that is, of almost no color at all, unless one is compelled to observe the lurid shades of the Blackmurian style." This was written in affection, Tate confessing that he had been "for a long time" on Blackmur's side and hankering to see himself as a horse of no color. Primary colors addicted him, though, and he said he couldn't pretend to ever having had a side his friend Blackmur could be on. He was wrong about this.

\*     \*     \*

Allen and Richard had begun corresponding in 1929, and Allen in the thirties had boosted Richard for the Guggenheim grants that got him started on his life of Henry Adams. A phrase of Donald Davidson's—he was Paean General for all the Fugitives—says how they joined hands. They were still Rebels, still Yankees, each passionately loyal to a cause irretrievably lost. Each of them presents the King over the Water, a phrase Richard used when, making one of his mistakes, he dismissed the novels of Ford Madox Ford. Or they present the outsider—animated, Richard said, "by loyalties and consciences utterly alien to the life and society in which they find themselves." Tate's loyalties were Southern, but "there is a New England, too," Richard reminded him, "with the ruin of unused or deprived possibility in her bowels." Sometimes loyalty in Tate was endearing; sometimes it gave scandal. When he talked about Gettysburg and how the rebel charge broke against the bayonets of Stannard's Vermont brigade, tears filled his eyes. This was endearing. But Tate on his native grounds was less endearing than abrasive. Homosexuality brought him to a boil—as when Allen Ginsberg came to lecture at Vanderbilt—and he made it an emblem for what was wrong with modern times. (Robert Frost was the same.) Stokeley Carmichael, a demagogue, came to Vanderbilt too. He touched off a ruckus in the black community; and this, Tate supposed, was the end of the world. "The negro race," he said, "is an inferior race." But he wrote in "The Swimmers," one of the permanent American poems, an absolute account of a lynching remembered from his boyhood in Kentucky.

Tate wrote his poem in terza rima, hard going in English. "The paucity of English rhymes leaves it clumsy and monotonous in all but the hands of a master. Shelley tried it once with moderate success." (Here Professor X bolted for the doors, and that was Allen's polemical intention.) MacLeish in the thirties had tried the form too. But Allen, reviewing MacLeish's *Conquistador*, said: "The refinement of the craftsmanship hovers over a void." In his own poem he filled the void with compassion. That sounds a little plummy-abstract, and anyway more needs to be said. First of all this poet paid honor to language, and the meticulous honoring by which you recognize his poetry and prose covers a multitude of sins. What was controversial in Tate, Richard said, was often a matter of temperament or temper. "There is a strength to his language superior to any ideas that may be detached from it."

Among poets of his own generation, the one Tate ranked highest was Crane, the homosexual. He loved the poetry; he also loved Crane the man. The violence of modern life was his special abhorrence, but in his cups he spoke equably of the murder of JFK. Sometimes it seemed to him that Jews were latecomers and not quite American. But racial prejudice moved him to public confession. "I have felt it," he said, "and felt humiliated by it." In 1943 he addressed a public letter to the poet Karl Shapiro "from a past remotely different from yours, from a radically different conception of the history and destiny of this country of ours." Never mind the difference—"the common humanity of poets" wasn't founded in shared political or social persuasion. It was founded in "that final honesty which is rare, unpleasant, and indispensable in a poet of our time." Striving for this honesty, Tate said he had failed to achieve it. But Shapiro hadn't failed: "as I wish at this moment to acknowledge."

Remembering Allen Tate, you are driven back endlessly on qualification. Otherwise you miss him, a huddle of contradictions both splendid and sorry. "Unlike her contemporaries," he wrote of Emily Dickinson, "she never succumbed to her ideas." Sometimes it was nip and tuck for both, though. This is true also of R. P. Blackmur, the parti-colored man. Leslie Fiedler, meeting Richard for the first time in the early fifties, was introduced by Saul Bellow. "We ended up sitting about talking and especially drinking." With Richard the two went together. "Bellow had predicted that when he got to a certain point of drunkenness, Blackmur would begin an anti-Semitic tirade, which in fact he did." Fiedler didn't know "even in retrospect" how much Richard believed in what he was saying or how much he was having on his liberal friends. I suspect the latter, Fiedler suspecting that "he didn't know himself." Blackmur the compulsive anti-Semite, roused to nasty remarks in the presence of Jewish friends, reappears in Fiedler's short story "Pull Down Vanity!" The title suggests a point of view. But Fiedler was aware how Richard's feelings about Jews were complicated and contradictory, the milk of human kindness mingling with a surfeit of bile. "He needed to have them near him," feeling more at home with Jews "than with other fellow writers and teachers."

Tate's Fugitive politics, said his friend Tom Mabry, had "no spiritual significance for the majority of people, whose social and economic inheritance grows increasingly urban." But what was a Fugitive, Tate wanted to know, and he answered: "quite simply a Poet: the Wanderer, or even the Wandering Jew, the Outcast, the man who carries the secret wisdom around the world." In his essay on *Ulysses*, Richard said that the Jew is Everyman the outsider and that, "in each of us, in the exiled part, sits a Jew." Richard was a Fugitive. Politics for both Richard and Allen rises from and comes down to a sense of the alienated self. This makes the formal stance a matter of indifference. Neither had much to say for President Roosevelt. They resemble Roosevelt, however, preoccupied on the eve of D-Day with the fortunes of a former servant who had gone off to the war.

Each admired Baudelaire, but neither cared for the poetè maudit. Each distrusted man in the natural condition. "Redemption might be possible for individuals," Tate said, "but the state was beyond redemption, and nature was evil." Each studied punctilio. "In essential forms of conduct" conventionality, Richard said, was the thing. Aware that manners made the man, he wasn't aware how sometimes they were simple evasion. His high-toned manner made you think of what Emerson said about Thoreau—that you would sooner embrace an oak tree than take hold of his hand. "Dancing with Dick," a woman said to Malcolm Cowley, "was like dancing with a steel cable of the Brooklyn Bridge." Tate around women was easier than this (to understate a little.) His lifelong friend Donald Davidson, having married only once, looked at Allen askance. "I was Don Davidson's purple patch," he said complacently. But no more than with Richard did you presume with Tate. Cowley thought he used politeness in defensive ways, and sometimes as an aggressive weapon against the stranger. He brandished this weapon in his polemical wars. He has kept up a running battle "this quarter century," Richard said, and might have been speaking of himself.

In the thirties, Richard and Allen celebrated each other at a distance. Richard wrote in praise of Tate's *Reactionary Essays*, and Allen doubted "if any writer of any sort, at any time in literary history," had ever received so nearly perfect a review. On Richard's achievement he went up and down. He said the criticism was the finest since Eliot's in *The Sacred Wood*. Some of the poems he called worthless pastiche; some he praised to the skies. The best of these poems, some a permanent part of our repertory, appeared in 1937. *From Jordan's Delight* was the title Richard gave them, remembering an island off the coast of Maine. This volume, Allen said, constituted the best American poetry of the decade. Forty years later he hadn't changed his mind.

Richard stood to Allen like acolyte to master, the way Delmore Schwartz stood to Richard. Allen's mind attracted him powerfully as a type "because it integrates its insights at the level of experience." He came to see how this early judgment was partly fallacious, and later he said doubtfully that Allen rejoiced in "the power of received philosophy." As Richard got older and his critical talent began to shrink, the paler charms of philosophy attracted him too. In the mid-forties, his first sketch of "A Burden for Critics" gave Allen "more hope than anything you've done in several years," and he saw "enormous possibilities in this new *organon*." To the insights which came to Richard only as personal messengers, it would lend the support of "a schematic, or if you prefer, a philosophical structure." Shouldering the burden of received philosophy was uncongenial labor for Richard. Allen took it up cheerfully. John Crowe Ransom supposed he was looking "for something special in the aesthetic experience," where Ransom and Blackmur could "see only an ordinary scientific or animal core plus glittering contingency."

Tate found what he was looking for in *Symposium*, "the best critical quarterly published in America up to its time." You can understand why he said this. *Symposium*, like its editors Philip Wheelwright and James Burnham, was ideational-philosophical all the way. "There is in ideas," Burnham asserted, "in the most general ideas removed from immediate relations with contemporary events... an intrinsic interest that does not need defending." Tate approved this opinion, and faulted Blackmur for his want of "methodology." At the same time he understood a different want in himself. His "use of dogma" needed for completeness Richard's "powers of elucidation." Maybe one precluded the other.

They talked the matter out at Princeton. On fundamentals, Richard said, a gulf opened between them, Allen "being always instinctively on the side of the absolutist angels, I still lost on the provisional side. It is in this sense that he discounts my `philosophy.'" Richard held that his philosophy "is whatever it is"—like Eliot's remark that the only unity in Shakespeare was in the sum of his works. "I may change, or grow, or blow up," Richard said. In the meantime he was satisfied merely to "variegate about a cumulatively sedimenting norm." This didn't satisfy Allen. "Like many admirable minds," he was "absolutely scared and footloose (headloose)," Richard said, "if, for a moment even, he feels himself without the support of something that will do for a philosophy." Richard himself "almost" preferred the quicksands.

They hadn't met until the fall of 1938, when Richard's friend from early days, the poet Theodore Spencer, invited Allen to lecture at Harvard. Jack Wheelwright was in the audience—until he died he was the catalyst for Richard and had introduced him to Matthew Josephson, then Lincoln Kirstein, now Allen Tate. Robert Lowell was there, too—Caligula Lowell, Richard called him, the Emperor of Ice Cream. After the lecture Wheelwright brought Richard up to the platform. So Tate and Blackmur were face to face, an agreeable way to be for the two years they spent together at Princeton. But like the heads on Mt. Rushmore, they looked best to one another when seen from a distance.

\*    \*    \*

Allen had come to Princeton in 1939 from the Women's College at Greensboro, North Carolina. His job was directing a program in Creative Arts. Dean Christian Gauss, setting it up, wanted to put the creation of arts and letters on the same footing as the study of their history. Edmund Wilson, a former student, was the dean's first choice as director. But the English Department jibbed at the appointment. Wilson was too cantankerous, or he liked to drink, or else the cantankerous man had a scunner against Princeton. That was Allen's opinion, ventured with a straight face. In any case the job fell to him, not to Wilson. A year later he got the college to hire Richard as his assistant. This, he said, was how the cuckoo got into the nest.

Blackmur's colleagues at Princeton were looking for a cicerone who could walk their students through the mysteries of modern literature. Tate might have been the man, but he let them down badly. Invited to give a talk to the English department, what he gave was "Miss Emily and the Bibliographer." Miss Emily is Faulkner's heroine who murders her lover and conceals the dead body in the bedroom. This was grim but not so grim, Allen supposed, as what his academic hosts were doing all the time. "Better to pretend with Miss Emily that something dead is living than to pretend with the bibliographer that something living is dead." The pretending explained the phrase, widely current among scholars, "the corpus of English literature." This phrase was their way "of laying literature out for burial." So Allen prepared his departure from Princeton. "That night," said the secretary of the English Club— it was he who had issued the fateful invitation and the memory of what occurred made him quiver as he spoke—"That night—Allen Tate—showed himself—in all ways—a cad."

Blackmur also was a cad in this academic sense of speaking your mind, but never so entangled as Tate in his beliefs or so aggressive in standing for them. You do not hear him whistling "Dixie" ("I'll Take My Stand") or challenging H. L. Mencken to a duel. Also, said his friend, he made a cunning politician: he "connived" was the way Allen put it. This seems very doubtful, not in the nature of the beast. Richard said he expected to depend on Allen "for orders and aids." But he had to dispose of his rivals, Allen said, and the deference was only a blind. When Jacques Barzun in a book review called Allen a fascist, Richard in mock sympathy went to Dean Gauss. "Allen isn't really a fascist," he said. This malicious anecdote strengthened with time. Later Tate had Richard saying: "Allen isn't a Nazi, just a Nazi sympathizer." Sequentially or not, and after three years at Princeton, Tate found himself out of a job.

Between Allen and Richard there was never a formal occasion of war, and what happened in Princeton is mostly the embittered, so distorted, creation of memory. Richard said to Allen: "Violence is always inexplicable; it is the gap between words; between actions." The changing of the guard went without incident, and Allen and Richard continued to send friendly letters back and forth. They worried about the war. Allen was too old for military service, but should Richard be drafted he might be sent for training to one of the southern camps, Forrest or Oglethorpe. That would put him within visiting distance of Monteagle, the mountain community in middle Tennessee where Allen and Andrew Lytle had established a permanent base. (Andrew had the Stars and Bars plastered across the front of his cabin.) They didn't meet in Monteagle, but they kept together, in Richard's phrase, on the longest slopes of the mind.

In their letters they swapped opinions on poetry, and Richard gave his opinion that Tate wrote better poetry than he did—"of another and more valuable (more deeply useful, referential) magnitude." That was what nineteen years of reading had told him. He concluded: "In this something less than human world I am all the more faithfully Yours and Caroline's." But Tate's anger was building. He had plenty of anger, and he stoked it for the rest of his life. In 1959 "Dick made partial amends." He paid his respects to "the different temperament of Tate—more active, more engaged, more cavalier" than his own. This ultimate tribute—meant, Allen said, "for my sixtieth birthday"—was "San Giovanni in Venere," St. John the ascetic tangled in the arms of Venus, Tate the ideologue secure in his beliefs, at the same time absurdly and triumphantly outside them in a violence of uncertainty and conviction. Tate's entire career validates this ambiguous character. He is to his fingertips the dogmatic and purposive man. He is also their antithesis, as when he discriminates the limitation of Edmund Wilson as a literary critic. For Wilson "the subject matter alone has objective status." The form the work takes is external, on Wilson's view, only mere technique. So the de-formed substance is correlated with its origin, in the elementary sense with its meaning, and critical thought becomes impossible. How, Tate inquired, does the moral intelligence get into poetry? He answered, "It gets in not as moral abstractions but as form, coherence of image and metaphor, control of tone and of rhythm, the union of these features." This is absolute criticism.

Tate has other ways of saying this, all of them right on the money. For example (speaking of T. S. Eliot and the movement in poetry he epitomizes): "the poetry is special, personal, of no use, and highly distinguished." Some critics denied the distinction, and Tate saw them as dominating our intellectual life. They were like the French mathematician who read a tragedy by Racine and wanted to know what it proved. Tate had an answer. He said: "It proves nothing; it creates the totality of experience in its quality; and it has no useful relation to the ordinary forms of action." This is a little didactic and possibly verbose. Here is a tighter and tougher version: "The better the art," Tate wrote, "the more pusillanimous. For art aims at nothing outside itself." What the art aimed at was Tate's entire business on his best or impersonal side. Tate the radically flawed man was after all aware, said his flawed panegyrist Blackmur, "of what is time out of mind in the movement of the hand or the reservation of the eye."

Allen was mollified a little, but rancor continued to run deep. He said of Richard the man: "I ended up disliking him." But he offered to introduce Richard's collected poems when posthumous publication was mooted in 1965. Tate's taste was deep too, and this required, as Richard said, "the love at the bottom of his contentiousness." Necessarily, rancor and love jostled each other. Tate's great men in modern letters were Eliot and Ransom, and when he lay dying, their photographs hung on the wall of his bedroom. "My two masters," he said. In this context he talked about early days, resuming his long career and his long and equivocal friendship with Richard. Finally he said: "He was our best American critic."

What did these critics have in common? Blackmur asked the question in "San Giovanni in Venere." His answer: "an ancestry of art for art," and "a belief in... the absolute sovereignty of poetry." Their undivided attention went to the "work in itself." It comprehended, said Tate, "the complete knowledge of man's experience." By knowledge he meant "that unique and formed intelligence of the world of which man alone is capable." The poem was a formal object in which "form is meaning and nothing but meaning." All roads led back to form.

The academic community denied this, and dissolved the poem into biography and history. It offered a pretext for the study of the sexual life of the poet, maybe of the reader, or anything else that

Professor X, pursuing his own vagaries, wanted to study. Usually, Allen said, he wanted to study anything but poetry. When he studied poetry, he put his mind to it, though. Mostly, that was all he did. Not attending much to what Richard called "the hymn in the throat," he thought the poem came down to ideas. His master critic was Plato, more likely one of the epigones more platonic than Plato, who spoke for the de-formed substance or ghostly paradigm of things. Ransom said of Plato in 1939, in his Phi Beta Kappa poem at Harvard: "We're in his shadow still." The principal achievement of New Criticism was to get us free of this shadow. The New Critic insists—following Blackmur—that what doesn't transpire cannot be said to have been experienced. He disbelieves in rationality as "the cumulus and discrimination of skills," and he tends to make "the analyzable features of the forms and techniques of poetry both the means of access to poetry and somehow the equivalent of its content."

This defines the New Criticism, which Blackmur and Tate created between them, applying it with a difference. The two of them as critic, Ransom said in the Thirties, "would make the best in the world." They never made this composite critic, but their difference notwithstanding they ate the same bread. There is the letter old Henry Adams wrote to Henry James, after the death of William James: "We all began together, and our lives have made more or less of a unity, which is, so far as I can see, about the only unity that American society in our time had to show."

# 9

# Delmore Schwartz and the Death of the Poet

Everybody called him Delmore. The friends who wrote about him after his death make you think that to know him was to love him. One of the friends, the philosopher William Barrett, said he was the most magical human being he'd ever known. For witty talk, said Tessa Horton—she painted Down East scenes with an eye to Correggio—no one came close. But it wasn't the wit that endeared him. He awoke a protective feeling in his friends. They wanted him to pull himself together, as perhaps in his place they would have done. Or putting it the other way, they wanted him to have what they sensed he didn't, the freedom to choose and the vitality to act on his choices. "He was a marvelous talker when well," said Tex Kaufmann, Delmore's colleague at Princeton, but otherwise "an emblem of anguish and saturate distress." This emblematic quality is one reason he survives. He is the good man beset, and he comes home more painfully, even at the remove of anecdotes and letters, than most people you meet every day.

Built-in problems are a drag on his story, making it hard for readers to keep going. Disasters were always raining on his parade, depressing us and risking fatigue. You know from the beginning that the hero is going to end badly. He is up there, like Empedocles, on top of the volcano, and it is only a matter of time before he jumps in. How do you fill out the time until then, and how do you achieve suspense when the ending is foreordained? This is the problem of tragedy, called inevitable when it succeeds, but also and paradoxically a fair fight that can go either way. Delmore's tragedy doesn't bear out the paradox. There is potentially a touch of morbidity, mounting to tedium, in following the fortunes of the man who never had a chance.

The work is a thornier problem. Time having winnowed it, just enough is left to make him worth retrieving, a handful of poems and one miraculous story. R. P. Blackmur, the doyen of New Criticism and another loyal friend, looked at the poetry in a letter of 1941. "I suppose you want complaints," he said to Delmore, offering a lot of them. But even a great poet must come in for his share, and Blackmur's complaints aren't that damning. The problem is the poetry's thinness. Blackmur's kind of meticulously analytical criticism, the kind that made him famous, doesn't find enough texture to work with. Compare, for example, early Blackmur on Wallace Stevens, a poet whose language often perplexes us but repays painstaking reading . James Atlas, Delmore's biographer, concluding the biography (1977) on an upbeat, suggests that the dead poet has returned to haunt the living. This is doubtful, if only the poems are in question. But though Delmore's achievement is small and mostly early, we remember the hero, more than what he made.

At Princeton in the early fifties, he was a cat among the pigeons. Sons of the rich and famous sat in his class, among them Harvey Firestone. Like Oscar Wilde, Delmore could resist anything except temptation, in his case the chance for a joke. "Mr. Firestone," he said, "I just had a flat tire." This got a laugh, but he played the biggest jokes on himself.

Princeton in his time split in two camps, high living and plain thinking. Delmore tilted toward both. He made a vow, he wrote to Blackmur: "I shall not cease from gentle fight/ Nor shall my glass slip from my hand,/ Till I have built Bohemia/ In Jersey's green and pleasant land." But another part of him, "Jewish-Presbyterian," stood outside bohemian Princeton. He had what solicitous people call "bipolar disorder." The mock-scientism would have tickled him, dressing up our common malady, "like a clown in regal purple dressed."

But it wasn't his two-in-one self that set him apart from others, even those who were intellectually and morally his superiors. The habit of poetry marked him or let us say dowered him, meaning that it was given, not earned. His peculiar gift, though not always fruitful, allowed him access to a dark river flowing beneath him. Like Dylan Thomas, who is describing his own activity as a poet, he could send down his bucket whenever he chose. Until he lost the habit, he kept sending it down, hoping for pearls or the truth Shakespeare's character thought was hid "within the center."

The resort of the poet to the hidden sources of things troubles the children of light. Their distrust of the children of darkness, the poet's party, is inveterate. Blackmur called the poet "the darkness shining in the light which the light cannot comprehend." He is blessed in what he confers but afflicted in what he knows. He can tell you "At the dark's edge how great the darkness is." That is Conrad Aiken, a better poet than Delmore. But each of them jeopardizes the social contract or social conspiracy. Orpheus, dismembered by the Thracian women, is the type of the poet.

And Delmore was a nice American boy. The auspices weren't right for tragedy. As a boy he played sports and got into fistfights. He loved baseball, and when he was fourteen his "entire attitude toward existence" was transformed by the trade which brought Rogers Hornsby from the Cards to the New York Giants. At Yaddo, the writers' colony in Saratoga Springs, he admired dutifully the winter sky, "crowded with the stars in constellations" (poetry), but what was on his mind was the sports pages of the *World-Telegram* and news from the hot stove league. Later he asked himself: "Why don't I feel the same intensity about the writing of poems as I do when I root for the Giants against the Dodgers?"

As a student he was only so-so, and this endears him too. He read a lot but pleased himself, finding it hard to knuckle down to close study. A friend said he lacked *sitzfleisch*. On the other hand, he believed devoutly in the American idea that if you applied your-self, rewards were sure to follow. Edison, the type of dogged appli-cation, was an early hero, so was Lucky Lindy. They represented, said Delmore, "the paradigm of his future success." Maybe a warn-ing flag ought to go up here. In his time of trouble he wrote to Blackmur, "I have a new sentence for my tombstone: 'Diligence is not enough.'" A comment of his on what goes with being a poet sums up his early career: "The poet wishes to establish these obser-vations, feelings, etc., *outside* himself once and for all, in the full light, in a stadium from which the crowd never goes home." You know a man by the metaphors he uses.

This apprehensible Delmore, a man you can take hold of, might have been imagined by Norman Rockwell, i.e., first-rate draughtsmanship in the service of second-rate creations. But in his secret place he was an intellectual. At seventeen he was reading *Hound & Horn*, also Pound's Cantos as they came out, everything by T.S. Eliot. He never got free of Eliot's shadow. He loved the poet but hated the austere presence and the literary boss. He endowed the boss with a sex life. How had Eliot come to marry Vivienne Haigh-Wood? They were punting on the Cherwell in his Oxford days and Vivienne said to Eliot—Delmore had her say—"Put your pole in, Tom!" He did, and after that the only honorable course was marriage. The scurrile stories Delmore invented made him feel guilty, as what didn't? He dreamed that Eliot had rejected his writing and had visited him in a peep show. So Eliot became "peeping Tom."

Pound was another equivocal master. He hated Pound's anti-Semitism but was able to accommodate it, partly because his sense of not belonging transcended his Jewishness. He wore Jewishness like a metaphor. He was the "Imaginary Jew" of John Berryman's short story, "the excluded stranger passing under the lighted window." Blackmur said: "In each of us, in the exiled part, sits a Jew: the darkness which the brightness does not comprehend." Delmore was an exile even when he was a literary lion and the foundations were dumping money in his lap. "In my young youth," he wrote Blackmur, "when I went to four different universities, God only knows why, I did not ever perceive that nobody liked Jews because not only was I not asked to join the Aryan fraternities, I was not asked to join the non-Aryan ones."

His great hero was Joyce, who fashioned his soul in exile and cunning. His great book was *Finnegans Wake*, the hermetic book to end them all. Only an adept could read it. Delmore was an adept. He called his cat Riverrun, after the first word in Joyce's novel. But Delmore was a democrat too, and he responded with fellow feeling to this author who loved the world and all quotidian business. He wrote subsequently,

> I think maybe an artist's faculties
> Can function at their best only if caught,
> Caught like a forest in a blazing fire
> Only if drawn into the age itself.

He was wary of the age, however, and chose to look on without committing himself, like Peeping Tom. In the thirties he translated Julien Benda, author of the famous *Trahison des Clercs*. The treason of the intellectuals was commitment to the world. He saluted Benda's plea for intellectual disinterest. He was human, and a bundle of contradictions.

His deepest commitment was to poetry, except that he had a wandering eye. All things could tempt him from the craft of verse. This was to his credit, but only as a man. He wanted to be a rentier, he told Aileen Ward. At Harvard Graduate School, where he studied philosophy, he dreamed of the good life presented by Renoir in his *Luncheon of the Boating Party*. He was one of the party, surrounded by pretty women on the sunny terrace overlooking the water. Meanwhile philosophy was left to shift for itself. But some of his dream he translated to fact.

He became the cynosure in the painting. In the summer of 1935, on a weekend in July, he wrote the short story which made him famous and on which his future fame as a writer will depend. This story, "In Dreams Begin Responsibilities," Nabokov called one of his "half a dozen favorites in modern literature." Delmore was twenty-two and never wrote as good a story again. He is Irwin Shaw's hero in "The Eighty Yard Run." But that isn't wholly accurate. He did really score once in the stadium from which the crowd never goes home.

His masterpiece appeared in *Partisan Review*, which gave it pride of place over contributions by Wallace Stevens and Edmund Wilson. His first book of poems, published by New Directions in 1939, made *Harmonium* and *Leaves of Grass* look like nothing. Anyway, his reviews let him think so. Blackmur found in this collection "inexhaustible quality." Tate invoked for comparison Eliot and Pound. He said Auden was a camp follower, compared to Delmore. All that was lacking was a plug from Al Schweitzer: "Not since the Bay Psalm Book...."

If you climb up so high when you're young, how do you stay there or how do you find the grace to get down? "All these fine reviews," Delmore wrote to his publisher Jay Laughlin, "are accumulating to the point where I am going to be terrified. It can't last." It didn't last. The rest of Delmore's life—he lived into his fifties and died in 1966—constitutes a footnote to his early promise. First his writing failed. He was the subject he couldn't exorcise. The verb says he was possessed. In an early draft of his second book, *Genesis*, he wrote: "Who am I? is the leading question." He asked this question interminably, and his public got bored and fell away. But he never had much of a public. He sent a copy of his first book to his brother Kenneth, and Kenneth wrote back to say that he had

"liked the book very much except for the fact that I don't like poetry as I can't understand it. I showed it to a few people and they
were very much impressed except for the fact that they didn't have
$2.50 they would have bought the book."

Delmore at forty compared his thoughts to "caravans of camels
lurching slowly across the seemingly endless Sahara." This metaphor defines his book of poems and stories, *The World Is a Wedding*, published in 1948. Turning the pages of the Talmud, he had
found the title "amid much trash and protocol." He asked himself
what this sentence could mean and he offered endless variations:
"the world is a misalliance, the world is a marriage of convenience,
the world is a shot-gun affair, the world is a royal match; one might
continue forever." So he ran up and down the hills and dirt roads of
his sensibility, and increasingly this was felt as agitation to no purpose.

Then he racked his body. He was an insomniac and addicted to
drugs, later to alcohol. At night he had to climb a peak from which
he jumped to sleep. Among his friends was Philip Horton, the biographer of Hart Crane and second husband of Tessa, the painter.
Already in the forties, Horton saw the desperation growing.
"Delmore," he wrote to Blackmur, "is stepping up his intake of
nembutal night by night." Through his suffering, he came to new
knowledge of Eliot. "'Trembling at dusk,'" he said, "is obviously
the trembling which begins at dusk before the first drink." A friend
observed him in these years, awkward, running to fat, his face
"coarsened by drinking." This face in old photographs is the beautiful face of the archetypal Romantic poet, "flagrant," said John
Berryman, "with young male beauty."

He had married his high school sweetheart Gertrude Buckman,
just like the silver screen, and now his marriage fell apart. Inform-
ing Blackmur of their separation, he wrote of his loneliness: "everyone is gone into the world of light and I alone sit lingering here—
with memories." Incoherence overtook him. The brilliant
conversationalist perceived "everything at once" and wanted "to
say it all at once." Descending on Blackmur one night in the Fifties,
he talked about "God knows what!—every mixed and unfinished
fragment of experience and autobiography and possibility he could
cram into the mass of six hours."

His friends were still willing to listen—loyalty to Delmore was their stock in trade—but he quarreled with them and drove them away. William Barrett remembered the self-destruction in his eyes, "always so expressive, gloating now in self-recrimination for his own evil." His second wife, Elizabeth Pollet, became the object of violent and insane repudiation. He imagined her having an affair with Nelson Rockefeller. He got put into Bellevue. When he came out, he hid himself in New York City and shifted from one sordid room to another. Robert MacGregor of New Directions glimpsed him briefly in 1959: "I ran into Delmore last Saturday morning at the corner of Sixth Avenue. He looked worse than I think I've ever seen him, his face lumpy and shapeless and the area around his eyes looking almost as if he had been in a violent brawl. At first it looked as if he were not going to speak, but then as we passed, suddenly, with an effort of concentration, he yelled something about jail. My companion afterwards said that he had said, "You're going to jail, Bob!" It was a little bit like a medieval curse. I guess I wasn't so much unnerved by it as depressed at the terrible human waste." The waste is terrible but fascinating. Delmore's last years are predicable of his earliest years, so the auspices weren't wrong after all.

\* \* \*

Delmore's story is tragic because it runs in a line. Back where it starts, you can make out the cause that begets it. He came from a home whose horrors you have to laugh at if you are not going to weep. His mother said, when Delmore's brother married a gentile, "He would have been better off in Buchenwald." When Delmore announced his own marriage, Rose Schwartz threatened suicide. Her gift to Delmore was guilt. When she died he refused to go to her funeral, and this was her ultimate gift. He became Stephen Dedalus in his own eyes. "I'm a bad son," he said. Blackmur came to bail him out one night in Princeton. He was in the drunk tank. "Punish me," he said. "I'm guilty!" His father was an immigrant who pulled himself up by his bootstraps, the ad astra theme again. He made a pile but was improvident and lost it all in the Crash. Harry Schwartz was the parent who was never around, a philanderer and not at pains to conceal this, in unselfconscious ways a stand-up Jewish comedian. When young Delmore, reading Spengler, explained how the West was declining, his father retorted: "Things are getting better all the time!"

All his life, Delmore looked over his shoulder. His best story recapitulates the courtship of his parents. He is sitting in a movie, watching the tragedy build to its climax, and when Harry proposes marriage he jumps from his seat and cries out, "Don't do it! It's not too late to change your minds, both of you. Nothing good will come of it, only remorse, hatred, scandal, and two children whose characters are monstrous." This in its black way is funny, and what saves the story of Delmore from the tedium of case history is the risible eye he turned on his own disasters. He was a psychic cripple and knew it, and he made comedy of what he knew. He tried without success to pull himself together, as if he heard Creon saying, "Oedipus, pull yourself together!" He submitted to analysis but spent the whole time arguing theory with the doctor. "Delmore is crazy," said William Phillips, who ran the *Partisan Review*. "He pays money to teach the analyst his business."

Harvard, where he taught English A, "Bonehead English," was a disaster but seriocomic. He agreed with John Berryman, who found it "a haven for the boring and the foolish." Princeton wasn't much better. In the house of intellect, he was starving for intellectual meat and drink. This bad joke aggravated his loneliness. Ezra Pound said he had tried for ten years "to get any member of an American faculty to mention any other member of his same faculty, in his department or outside it, whose intelligence he respects or with whom he will discuss serious matters in the university." Delmore knew better than to discuss serious matters in the university. He likened himself to a clown or burlesque queen, and joked about the student who wrote in her paper: "A liberal education makes a girl broader," or the student who quoted "Prufrock": "Shall I part my bare behind?" He stole this last from Phil Horton.

The fixity of purpose he saw in his academic colleagues depressed him. They kept their nose in a book, so had little to say. This was just as well. Also they were men of one idea, generally bad. He told how he had gone into a bookstore, "and discovered going from book to book that I have a sensibility that can be violated by any idea." This put him "at the North Pole from St. James," patron saint of the impersonal artist, aloof from his fictions like the God of the Creation.

But James's inviolate sensibility hinted at dark sexual desires. Delmore argued his point from the names of characters in the novels—Fanny Assingham in *The Golden Bowl*, Caspar Goodwood in *The Portrait of a Lady*, Mrs. Cundrip (he called her) in *The Wings of the Dove*. He thought it would be fun to have a masquerade party in memory of James. "Perhaps," he wrote to Blackmur, "we could get Philip Horton to play Merton Densher, Gertrude would be here as what Maisie knew, John Berryman could come as Roderick Hudson, Harry Levin"—a supercilious professor who fingered objets d'art—"as Gilbert Osmond, Helen (Blackmur) as the actress in *The Tragic Muse*, Edmund Wilson as Henrietta Stackpole, Eileen Berryman as Milly Theale simply because she has beautiful red hair. Tessa could be the spoils of Poynton, I would be present as Edith Wharton, and you could come as R. P. Blackmur."

Living in Cambridge, he recited Valéry to get himself up in the morning, never mind the hangover or the depression that was more cause than effect. "Il faut tenter de vivre." This sounded stoical-Romantic, and he modified it later. It "has now become—il faut get out of the pajamas every other day." He hated to travel, and he died without having been to Europe. "How could I go to Europe," he said, "when I can't even shave at home?" He tried writing plays but wasn't much as a playwright. But he didn't protest the crassness of the theater world. He meditated instead a play about "a colony for sexual happiness." He was going to call it: *Violated in the Vatican, Shamed in Chicago, A Pass in El Paso.*

His sexual life was no joke, though. He was endlessly promiscuous and he moved from bed to bed without apparent relish. He said, however: "When a man seeks different girls, he affirms his belief in the existence of the external world." This you have to cheer. Also he said he wanted to be married at the same time to Helen Blackmur and Tessa Horton. He decided it wouldn't work out. He remembered how Tessa's first husband had stepped into a dish of ice cream hidden under her bed ("thus summing up all possible marriages to Tessa"), and he wrote to propose that if they lived a second time, he should be the first to step into her dish of ice cream. "What flavor?" she asked him. "Tutti frutti," he said.

His marriage to Gertrude was heading for the rocks, so was John Berryman's marriage to Eileen, and he turned it to laughter in his "Doggerel Beneath the Skin":

All poets' wives have rotten lives,
Their husbands look at them like knives
   (Poor Gertrude! poor Eileen!
   Never more seventeen!)
Exactitude their livelihood
And rhyme their only gratitude,
Knife-throwers all, in vaudeville,
They use their wives to prove their will.

The jokes kept coming, but his writing was ancient history twenty years before he died. He said: "Sound judgment (and conquered neurosis and overcome evil) are the ground and fountain of writing well." His judgment worsened, his neurosis was on him like the mark of Cain, and in the end his own evil met the evil in the world. William Barrett inquired, in his memoir of Delmore, "when you add it all up, what have you?" and answered: "not something at all negligible.... But just as certainly a failure—and a failure all the more in relation to the power of the original gifts. It is that human failure that currently invokes the facile image of the *poète maudit*—the poet exiled and accursed by the tribe." The human failure is notorious. No one will doubt it, now that the file is closed. But Delmore the symbol is bigger than his file, and I have more to say about both.

*　*　*

The poet who labors under a curse sounds like a Romantic copout. The curse is real, however, and vivid in the roll of poets in their misery dead. Society's hatred requires the death of the poet. This hatred is from old times, for the gadfly that drives Io to frenzy or the scourge that drives the moneychangers from the temple. It isn't national, as when tiresome people indict America for the death of Dylan Thomas: "You killed him. In your God Damned Brooks Brothers suit." The hatred is racial, like the bosun's for Billy Budd. He has a daily beauty in his life. Also, in his poetry he poaches on forbidden ground. Donald Hall says, in his memoir of Dylan Thomas: "To make poems is to add metaphors of the forbidden child to words of the rational adult, making a third thing, which enlarges human consciousness." The child-adult dichotomy sounds modern and trendy, but not the enlarging, genuine, scary too. Plato, fearing it, banished the poets from his ideal society. Think it over, and you will sympathize with him.

What the poet makes displaces air—the living man in his habit who is so much more than the ideal man—so moral judgment goes out the window. Compunction goes with it. The poet's eye is on the manage of his craft. Like Orpheus, he kills his wife by turning around to see if she likes his singing. He is right to do this. Pound says: "Technique is the test of sincerity." Still, you can't quarrel with the women who tear him. That is what the world thinks. But the poet does too, on his Platonic or censorious side. He wasn't raised in the world for nothing. So, like Oscar Wilde, he punishes himself for his arcane commitment. In his own person he devours the god. He is Orpheus and Dionysus, he is also the avenging women, and in this sense his end is appointed: "thereof comes in the end despondency and madness."

Poetry is the moat, Harry Crosby wrote in his diary—he was only a soi-disant poet—and beyond is the world "that must be continually beaten back, the world that is always laying siege to the castle of the soul." But it isn't the world, it is the poet who puts the castle under siege. He makes a blasphemous religion of art, all hush and inutility, and complains of country ants who do their harvest offices. Or else, like John Synge, he sees between the peasantry and men of genius like himself, "an ungodly ruck of fat faced, sweaty headed swine." That is a hell of a thing to say, the more intolerable for being true. His peculiar quality, Blackmur said, is "insolence of spirit against the world." Blackmur means this for praise, so shows you his own descent from the men of the Nineties, who looked at the world through a lorgnette. But the greatness that distinguishes the poet from society overwhelms him in the end. "It is one of the characters of such greatness—of all greatness maybe—that it is the most easily destroyed."

The world is a wedding, full of loud bassoons, and the poet is the unbidden guest. He comes to the wedding like Randall Jarrell. "One felt, beside him, too corrupt and companionable. He had the harsh luminosity of Shelley, every inch a poet, and like Shelley, imperilled perhaps by an arid, abstracting precosity." Often, said Robert Lowell, in his tribute to his dead friend, "he seemed tone-deaf to the amenities and dishonesties that make human relations tolerable.... You felt that even your choice in neckties wounded him." It was as if he had made a compact with himself, "never to accept the bulk, confusion, and defeat of mortal flesh." The poet's "anguish and

saturate distress"—remembering a colleague's character of
Delmore—is partly in token of this compact. That is partly what I
mean in saying that his story runs in a line. His foolishness, like
everyone's, belongs to himself. Forget for the moment this com-
mon-garden foolishness. It isn't at issue here. God knows what
vulgar foolishness Shakespeare allowed himself or was constrained
to allow in his everyday character of mere shifter of scenes. "For
every man with his affects is born," says Berowne in *Love's Labour's
Lost*. These affects or inherited frailties are mastered not by striving
but by special grace.

Sometimes Delmore's foolishness verges on corruption. This I
lay to his genes, his want of moral character, also to his alienation.
He doesn't have a patch on his friend John Berryman, a braggart, a
drunk, a womanizer, a buffoon, and the author of "Winter Landscape." The relation is obscure but I make it out as contingent.
Berryman lived without hope and ridden by irrational fears. He
feared even the arrival of the daily mail. But he said: "We must
travel in the direction of our fear." This resembles him to all poets,
encounterers of darkness.

The encounter is painful, and hence the desire to escape, hence
alcohol and silence and the self-hatred that goes with it. The poet
may be God-bitten but can't rest in the ordinary way on the conso-
lations of religion or a secular religion, the panaceas that sustain
the rest of us if we are lucky. In a time when "the American poet
has come to enjoy almost no immediate audience," Berryman offered his definition of the motive for poetry: "a passion for getting
things right... a jealousy for the national honor... pity, outletting
agony or disappointment, exasperation, malice, hatred... the consciousness of a final two." Poetry, he said, "is a terminal activity,
taking place out near the end of things." His passion or exasperation impelled him to journey to the end of things. Not everyone
wants to go with him.

For his twenty-fourth birthday Dylan Thomas wrote a poem:

> In the groin of the natural doorway I crouched like a
>   tailor
> Sewing a shroud for a journey.

He meant that he was doomed from the beginning, and the event
proved him right. Here are other items in sequence. Berryman said:

"I have the authority of suffering." In particular he suffered from petit mal, a caricature of the divine fury with which the poet is blessed or cursed. His involuntary passion corresponds to that *hysterica passio* that afflicted King Lear, who fell sick as society drove him away and who couldn't be held accountable when the antic fit was on him. Delmore, wanting to help Berryman to a job at Princeton, wrote to Blackmur, extenuating his friend's antics: "John loses his temper in arguments and behaves like a maniac and it is not his fault." There is the metaphor in Romans of the potter who shapes his clay (9: 21). Delmore approved it and you can see why. He saw himself shaped for a vessel of wrath. This cleared him, he supposed, of personal responsibility.

Partly St. Paul's mysterious point is that personal responsibility remains. Delmore betrayed his talent. It is well to insist on this. Dylan Thomas collaborated in his death. Harry Crosby blamed everyone, excepting himself, and when he committed suicide he tied it to America, a country that stinks, he said, "of bananas and Coca Cola and ice cream." This got him off the hook. The poet John Wheelwright wrote about this event: "Poetry has saints. He was not of them. His death was his best poem." Berryman deserves a better epitaph than this but is culpable also, his "special malady" notwithstanding. He thought peace of mind was aloof from high art, so made a cult of desperation. His biographer Haffenden says: "The sense he always retained of himself as *maudit* led him to reflect by association on doomed figures like Peter Warlock, Hart Crane, Nijinsky, Bix Beiderbecke." This is bleakly comic, but has its other face. Think of Beiderbecke the non pareil, no one ever played better jazz trumpet than he did, going through the motions as dictated by Paul Whiteman, an affable version of the bulk, confusion, and defeat of mortal flesh. What will this mean, if your passion is for getting things right?

In an essay on "The Literary Life," Van Wyck Brooks regretted that only a handful of writers in his time had survived their first promise. He wanted to know what fate had overtaken the rest. "Shall I begin to run over some of those names, familiar to us all," the poets, novelists, and critics "who have lapsed into silence, or have involved themselves in barren eccentricities, or have been turned into machines?" He doesn't name names, but here are a few (coming down to the proximate past): Hart Crane, who jumped from the

stern of the steamship *Orizaba*; Dreiser, who took to the bottle; Ring
Lardner, who was sometimes observed alone, in the last months on
East Hampton, sobbing, with his face in his hands; Blackmur, a
walking thesaurus of medical ailments—he was the perfect host
and invited their company—who drugged himself to sleep with great
doses of bourbon; Nathanael West, born in the same year, who died
violently in his thirties, the day after his Hollywood neighbor Scott
Fitzgerald; Jarrell, who made poetry out of his loneliness until he
found it insupportable. "Poor modern-minded exile from the for-
ests of Grimm."

When Delmore was a student at New York University, one of the
way stations in his academic progress, he served as an editor of the
little magazine *Mosaic*, which featured in its brief existence a tribute to Norman Macleod, poetry by Blackmur, and a letter from
Pound. Put these three together and you have a fair composite of
the modern poet, what Delmore saw when he looked in the mirror
or the writing he saw on the wall. Pound spent his last ten years in
silence, revolving the question whether to live or die. He said at the
end, "Everything that I touch, I spoil." But he has these lines, in a
late Canto:

> A blown husk that is finished
> but the light sings eternal.

Blackmur lost the habit of poetry, and in his last years he turned
public and preceptorial. This, he said, was his next best substitute
for the head in the gas stove. At the end he was a ruin but he survived until the end. Macleod, who starved in the twenties, became
in the Thirties a well-known "older" poet. He is the nicest man of
the three. His allegiance was not primarily to poetry, though. He
wrote from abroad in 1932: "Paris is a beautiful city. But my ideology remains the same in spite of everything: Solidarity Forever Till
the Revolution comes." He repeated this litany three times in his
letter. It is his memorial, not poetry.

Delmore had his poetry, a thin oaten reed and nothing to back it.
He wasn't cut out for a stoic. Some of his best friends were Marxists but he wasn't really political. He brooded much on death and
he sought to order his death in a letter to Blackmur: "I will seek to
have 'Survival Was His Hobby' inscribed on your tombstone, if...

you promise to see to it that 'Metaphor Was His Salvation' is inscribed upon mine, should I put off the body of the darkness before you." He outlived Blackmur by one year, and in the end his poetry didn't save him.

# 10

## Austin Warren: American Baroque

"Brother Austin," Allen Tate called him, a joke meant in earnest. Austin himself initiated this mode of address, applied to friends in the confraternity he presided over as abbot. The friends were Brother Cleanth, Sister Tinkum (Mrs. Cleanth Brooks), Brother Allen. A new essay by T. S. Eliot was an Encyclical. It needed exegesis, and meeting the need he headed his letters from "The Oratory of SS. Basil and Gregory Nazienzen," not a made-up place, the chapel in his house in Ann Arbor. Leon Edel remembered the chapel, a dim recess, icons on a low table draped with an altar cloth. The first time I called on Austin, summoned to the stone house on Oakland Avenue near campus, I took the highball he handed me and plunked it down on his altar. Our budding friendship almost ended right there.

It began in the sixties when I came to Michigan—he would have said and did say when I got the "call," not a phone call. In this academic venue where they laid out the "corpus" of letters, he showed like bright metal on a sullen ground. He cared about poetry, rare in English departments, and spoke without embarrassment of prayer. "Tomorrow is the Feast of Corpus Christi; pray for me."

The Eastern saints and icons locate him in his Greek Orthodox phase, among the varieties of religious experience that went to form an American original. He liked "heart-religion," also controverting the finer points of divinity, sport for a thinking man. The Methodist Christianity he got from his parents, only a higher prudence, "offered little to stir the imagination of the young"—I am quoting from his life of Henry James the Elder, like many biographies a version of its author—and failed altogether to quicken "the impulse to high deed and self-forgetful purpose." So in his teens he became a "Jesus-freak," then a Swedenborgian who detected connections between the soul and the natural kingdom. In adulthood, carrying this baggage with him, he joined the Anglican Church. A village librarian he knew, "of sharp mind and sharper tongue," claimed the right to shift her pew from the Congregational Church to the Episcopalian when the counsels of either displeased her, and this crotchety woman gives Austin's likeness too.

He mustn't be thought of as eclectic, however—magpies are that—and whatever the nomenclature he owed allegiance to a single religion. His laid hold "upon the heart, upon life," both terms asking attention. Beginning at home but self-forgetful, the religion he practiced meditated high deeds and didn't bring peace but a sword. It didn't pull a long face either. "John the Baptist with a sense of humor," he called James the Elder, a minatory prophet who hectored the rest of us, warning that the Day of the Lord was at hand. But his prophecies, like Austin's, were not less insistent "for the jocular idiom," or you could put this the other way round.

The autobiography, taking him up to his fortieth year, "nel mezzo del cammin," suggests his special quality, vintage New England filtered through other places, some exotic. An education-of-the-hero book, this account of gearing up resembles Milton's at Horton but isn't all "pre-'Lycidas'" and before you finish a modern hero comes into his own. Self made, he forged his soul when others weren't looking. Yankees did for themselves, and his birth on the Fourth of July—pinpointing the time, he said it occurred while the village parade was passing—chimed with his independent spirit. Anyway, this Swedenborgian saw a "correspondence."

His early, unloved youth tried him in a crucible he could have dispensed with. On the farm at Stow, his father coped "variously," his mother kept her distance, but he got along with the cows. No soulmates smoothed his way and some persecutors blocked it, like the local bully who beat him up at school. One of his teachers, "utterly, painfully, New Englandly conscientious," made him hate Shakespeare, not easy. The plays, said Austin ruefully, helped you parse old English words. Wesleyan College, entered by him without expectations, didn't disappoint. Hiding out in the library, he instructed himself, though.

He didn't always elude academic tormentors, and later, at Harvard, awful G. L. Kittredge jumped him through hoops. Irving Babbitt at Harvard ("my one great 'official' teacher") spoke to him where he lived, or where one part of him did, and he warmed to Babbitt, and Paul Elmer More at Princeton. But these mentors and friends set snares for his feet. Both wanted disciples in the narrow church they belonged to, and "becoming what one is," the title of his memoir, he had to fight free of them both.

Searching for a vocation, he turned inevitably to teaching, his appointed role, and in his twenties recreated Little Gidding in rural New England. This was "the place you would be likely to come from" (remembering Eliot in *The Four Quartets*). An Arnoldian saving remnant, St. Peter's School admitted only the "elect." Like Austin's chapel in Michigan, it existed in time and space, "in eternity and ubiquity" too. Not everybody talks the way he did.

"Oral glibness," his own, often fooled him, however, and he needed pen and paper to show up "my incoherences." He said you couldn't be an honest teacher without finding time to write. (Facile proponents of "great" teaching unmediated by writing didn't hear him and still don't.) "To be, or to do, anything," you had to "give up almost everything," though, and his younger time shows him jettisoning cargo. A rigorous scholar himself, he looked mistrustfully at Professor X, "master of a single theme or the exposition of a single dead author—a life for a life." Right on target, that last bit, scathing talk from someone who earned it.

Disputing the received wisdom—it was all for pigeonholes—he wanted to be *ad omnia paratus*, "writing about what he was interested in writing about, and in whatever mode." This led to the study of comparative literature, an academic heresy still over the horizon when he got started. He "had the nerve to conceive of it" (said his friend Glauco Cambon) "as the normal horizon of critical inquiry," not another special "field" to be marked out and properly tagged. Once he told me, "You are a comparativist," adding, as he was. I cherish the likeness.

In the 1930s, throwing away the 3 by 5 cards, he set up as a critic. Next he dropped the formal lectures, turning his classroom into a happening. A scandal to the scribes, he asked students to close their notebooks and open their minds. In the photo on my office wall he stands silent before the class, lips pursed, eyes abstracted behind the thick glasses. This professor is evidently at sea. Much risk in letting them know that you don't know the answers, and most, dreading silence, fill it with words, words. A caption beneath the photo has Austin saying, however: "I want, in a sense, to teach something which I have not yet learned."

As this story ends, he has found his vocation, teaching the young who committed themselves to his "pastoral" care—that was how he put it—and reflecting in print on what he taught them. Twin pursuits, they kept him busy the rest of his life.

\* \* \*

The reflections move him a long way from his master Babbitt and the Neo-Humanist ensign he nailed to the mast. (Fluttering bravely, it went down with the ship.) A moralistic creed, Neo-Humanism held that our modern "decadence" represented a sad falling off. Rousseau, a famous decadent, laid the ax to our tree, but already you could see the rot setting in with Shakespeare. His *Antony and Cleopatra* balanced good and evil in too perfect an equipoise, like the swan's down feather lackeying the tide. Babbitt wished it would stick in one place,

Accommodating what the master called perverse or morbid, Austin made his own larger and scarier world. Or rather he lived it, exemplifying, said Philip Young, the Baroque in the flesh, "dramatic, jagged, genuine." Near the end of his life, he still found life complex, intolerably this, and kept trying to simplify in the interest of a harmony he knew in his bones was factitious. But ecumenicism, the real right catholic thing, forbade him to throw out the baby with the bathwater. "*Any* of the babies," he said.

His tolerance, different from Laodiceanism where you don't speak your mind, not having one or not giving a damn, begins with the scrupulous canvassing of fact. So many facts or figures in the carpet must postpone a rush to judgment, but first of all you have to entertain them. For the literary critic, Austin par excellence, this meant absorption in words. A "lay theologian" (self styled), he got his finicking preoccupation with words from teasing out occulted meanings in the Bible. The same myopic queerness—a vice, Dr. Johnson thought—describes Shakespeare.

Biblical exegesis, "the archetype of our literary 'close reading,'" flowered, Austin said, in hermeneutics, a science of the interpretation of texts. He saw how this science played into the "New Critical" study of literature, and I see him myself as an etymologist, though raised to the nth power, with connections to Ransom, Blackmur, and Tate. Among his antecedents is the early Christian exegete, Isidore of Seville. He wrote an *Etymologies* too.

Dusted off in recent days, hermeneutics, new style, is one of modern theory's buzzwords, and gives an infinite range of meanings their charter. Purporting to deal with poetry, it pirouettes about the poem, doing what it can to keep from closing with the thing itself. Fear inspirits its little dance, possibly hatred, the fear at any rate having grounds. Words "slip, slide, perish, Decay with imprecision," and getting them right is work for intellectual athletes. Sometimes old Isidore, grappling with words, burned his fingers.

But hermeneutics in its accepted sense, while it allows of multiple meanings—and how should it not, truth being in the cards—stipulates their finite character. For determining the range, artistic intention is the sine qua non. Often ambiguous, this gleam in the artist's eye isn't unknowable but the reader who hopes to spot it must keep his own eyes on the page. He isn't all-in-all sufficient ("The Critic As Artist"), and *id est* is how he deals with the text.

Readers in our time when literary criticism, freed of its tether, runs down hill like the Gadarene swine, will find it useful to look into Austin Warren. Close reading is his benchmark, meaning honesty, meaning infinite patience, and of course he became a New Critic. Reared to his shame by ideological critics (he confessed to Blackmur in a letter of 1940), he said how "in the last five years, my association with poets and my own dissatisfaction at so external a way of dealing with poetry"—sociology and all that—"have turned me to very different methods." Nowadays his own teaching was largely in the spirit of *Understanding Poetry*, Brooks' and R. P. Warren's manifesto to the classroom. These preceptors and their New Critical colleagues took the line from St. John's Gospel for their point of departure. "In the beginning was the Word."

*Theory of Literature* (1942), the influential primer Austin made with Rene Wellek, displays his different methodology, not an ideologue's but pragmatic. More than any other work, said Allen

Tate, it civilized the teaching of literature. "Wellek & Warren" stated the obvious, rather like the Declaration of Independence. E.g. "The natural and sensible starting-point for work in literary scholarship is the interpretation and analysis of the works of literature themselves." To beneficiaries after the fact, it sounds ipso facto, but fifty years ago it brought down the house of index cards. Today when old corruptions titivated with new labels are back in the market, the obvious truth needs restating.

Only the works, said these urbane revolutionaries, "justify all our interest in the life of an author, in his social environment and the whole process of literature." Professors of literature, hunting ideas, preferred an all-around-the-barn mode of study, however. Students, hungry sheep who looked up but weren't fed, paid the price for this. "Confronted with the task of actually analysing and evaluating a work of art," they didn't know where to begin.

Yes, and I still get red in the face, remembering the first time I tried. "Sa vie et son oeuvre" gave the sense of Eng Lit when I went to school, and anecdotes, some entertaining, set the poet before us. Or Professor X, consulting his Tillyard, he of the Elizabethan World Picture, filled in the cultural "surround." Nothing wrong with the latter nor with the scholar who expounded it, except that both took the background for foreground. Explicating the text whiled away time, but knowing the background unlocked the heart of the mystery.

*Theory of Literature* changed all that. But it didn't propose that we read in a vacuum, the vulgar canard detractors lay at New Criticism's door. Ignorant of the significant past, American college graduates—a sorry bunch, Austin thought—forfeited "their preferred share in civilization." He and friends meant to reclaim it. Blackmur and Burke, two of the friends, knew more of our inheritance than any Ph.D. But they knew it on their pulses and inert knowledge didn't suffice them.

Meanwhile, Professor X guarded the portals. Easy to dismiss him, an amiable woolgatherer chomping on his cigar. But his bite was worse than his bark. At worst a "bookful blockhead," at best an appreciator who appealed to the viscera, he lacked the critical faculty, so forgot the original motive of knowing. What was that? Austin asked (in an essay mediating between the scholar and critic), and answered: to understand and apply. You see how his religion, personal plus social, dictates his critical stance.

Canonizing knowledge, he said the critic without background can never transcend journalism. "But without consciousness of a foreground in which men live and act he remains an *erudit*." From my "phylactery" I offer this, of Bernard Shaw's: "Beware of the merely learned man. He is an idler who kills time with study." So down with "disjecta membra," eye against hand and hand against heart. This New Critic has a watchword: "only connect."

Style enforced the connections, a point lost on primitivists who cry up the naked truth. "Plain, simple, sullen," Donne called this truth, indifferent to the niceties of language and unaware that nice isn't pretty but exact. Belletristic critics, the other face of a bad coin, thought a feast of language was better than enough. "Strike out every other sentence," Austin told them. Like Henry James (the Younger), he meant to cut off all "gracious twaddle."

Boiling down suited him, and the essay, not the book, is the form most in tune with his genius. Inscribing a copy of *The Elder Henry James* to Leon Edel, he said he longed to free this early work from verbosity, reducing the whole "to an immaculate 125 pages." He wanted only the essence, chapters condensed to paragraphs, paragraphs to a sentence. Each was a "topic sentence." Plunging straight in, he omitted the formal preface and ended without that conventional summary, dear to "Thus we see" writers. But he didn't appeal to "nuda veritas," no such animal, and another impulse opposes this centripetal one. He wanted his essays readable, not only about literature "but themselves literature." This second clause bespeaks a man with pretensions.

A mandarin of style, he cosseted words more than clarity needed, and that was New Critical too. His style, different from Blackmur's, convoluted, sometimes affected, edges toward the academy, like Tate's and Ransom's, all three university trained. But all have in common an uncanny sense of words as almost corporal entities. Being alive where the intellectual "message" is only matter-of-fact, they make a rival creation. More and more, this greatly aspiring writer came to see that the kind of meaning he aimed at, going beyond communication, incarnated itself in style: "and it is style— meaning in diction and rhythm—which is my final concern." Note the rhythm, important. Prose writers, those who matter, don't number syllables but not less than poets have a pattern before them, and the music counts as much as what they "say."

Not a critic by default (a failed poet or novelist) and unashamed of his profession, Austin called himself some kind of artist. "I would rather be a doorkeeper in the house of art than to dwell, all confidently and smilingly and blandly, in the courts of erudition and commerce." His friend Wallace Fowlie is putting words in his mouth. The words are stirring but don't claim enough for this humble yet proud man, and in the last chapter of the autobiography, "Becoming a Writer," he elevated his sights.

Though skilled in "practical criticism" where the self-effacing critic plays second fiddle to the artist, he found it easy "to slip into the view that novels exist in order that they may receive expert treatment; that poems exist in order that they may be interpreted." Then, flooring us, he says: "If *fin de siècle* poets could feel that the final end of the world is that it may all be taken up and consummated in a poem, I may be tempted to the view that the poem, in turn, is to be consummated by its absorption into a critical essay." The superbity astonishes—he himself feels its force and acknowledges a temptation that common sense will want to correct. However, the truth is out and stamps him a son of Oscar, after all the Critic as Artist. If I contradict myself in this portrait of him, then I contradict myself, and plead only that I take my lead from him.

\*   \*   \*

Like his life of James the Elder, his own biography "is properly and primarily that of a mind." But the mind, a house of many mansions, resists classification. He said of his hero and might have said of himself that his "independence, wit, and piquant idiom served to make him a subject for anecdotes." Over the years the anecdotes proliferated, some piquant like the idiom. They don't set him clear, though, and to express what he called "my stance" you need an "oxymoron," the rhetorical term he learned from his study of the Baroque sensibility. Illustrating, he drew his own ambiguous portrait: "an aristocratic noun or verb qualified but not wholly negated by its accompanying democratizing adjective or adverb."

Fastidious in person, this esthete walled off the world he lived in with books, music, and high talk. He had a rich baritone and kept and played a reed organ, his music, said Jack Wheelwright, "sprinkling silence over sound." A primitivist he wasn't, and while at St.

Peter's School thought of taking lessons in singing and dance. Neologisms cast him down, "realtor" for "real estate agent." Seeking the right nuance, his letters, sometimes precious, favor inverted commas. One, Henry Jamesian, tells of having "made an effort at 'games.'"

He wrote a crabbed hand, by far the worst George Core had ever tried to decipher. Receiving a letter, this editor of the *Sewanee Review* typed out all he could, then worked away doggedly at the lacunae. Highly speculative labor it was like cracking the Japanese code in wartime. But Austin wouldn't type his letters and wondered a little if you did. The typewriter intervened between friends.

No good himself at driving a car or cooking a meal, he thought teachers ought to cook and work with their hands. At St. Peter's, modeled on Brook Farm, they did this. He was the dean and saw to it. Religious but no quietist, he instructed his flock that politics and religion were "central modes of existential life." Grave but no Puritan, like the elder James he relished what the world had to offer: "good cigars, oysters, smart tailoring, books." Not a toper, he liked his drink, preferring dry martinis. Kenneth Burke recalled the two of them, arguing all night as they walked the dirt roads around Andover, New Jersey, breaking off for "alcoholic replenishment."

A generous critic, he was Chaucer's Clerk, fortified, said Edel, by an artist's discipline. Opening himself to friends who were writers, he corrected their prose in his great soft black pencil. Sometimes the Clerk was Cato the Censor, whose comments in the margin made you pale. "Mine is an irenic spirit," he asserted, but the peace-loving man had his swingeing side. If you crossed him he smote you. He had an aura too, adding cubits to his stature, also a large bump of ego. Woe to the friend who presumed.

The life, touched with greatness, mirrors the art, not always true of writers. "In me, from the start, have existed an artist (or at least an aesthete)," he said, "along with a moralist." Though the moralist was "sternest in self-judgment," that didn't preclude judging others. Abasing himself in a letter to Tate, he said we were all "poor, ignorant, sinful, lost, wavering and wandering creatures." Some wandered more than others, however. He looked down his nose at Blackmur, the autodidact who never made it out of high school. He himself was Dr. Warren, a Princeton Ph.D. Though disdaining academic credentials, he was willing to have it both ways.

"Literature *as such*" made a war cry or party-shibboleth on the Wellek and Warren side, an Iowa colleague remembered, and Austin, fixated almost comically on the figure in the carpet, comes close in his criticism to venerating art for its own sake. He wrote, however: "I distinctly do not believe that literature alone or as such is adequate for the salvation of mankind." "Our Jamesian traveler of the mind"—an apt phrase of Cambon's—wasn't about to succumb to Gilbert Osmond's temptation. Chasing salvation, he is the highest type of political man, i.e., engagé, and though harking back to the nineties, differs profoundly from ancestors like Pater and Wilde. Cain's chilly question: "Am I my brother's keeper?" would have seemed rhetorical to him.

"Our business," said his friend Jack Wheelwright, was "minding other people's." Like Old Testament Seth in Wheelwright's poem, Austin made wars to found or reconstitute the city wrecked by Cain. Alert to ends where most, missing the Pisgah-sight, care only for means, he undertook to see that we didn't board the wrong train for Beulah. "It may land you up in Englewood, New Jersey." Implacably serious, hence seriocomic, he raises eyebrows like Don Quixote. But he moves you to wonder, like Hamlet and Lear. In a world where all are on the make or take, he is our pole star.

*    *    *

There are more good poets than really competent critics, and Austin, being one of the latter, is rare. Before the twentieth century—"modern times"—I count half a dozen critics, erring if at all on the side of generosity, who still have something to say to us. Austin's place among practitioners of what Blackmur called the critic's job of work is just below the top tier. Part of that interlocking directorate of high-toned men of letters between the two World Wars and after—they found houseroom in quarterlies like the *Kenyon, Sewanee*, and *Southern* reviews—he helped make our criticism an art form. More than generals, CEOs, and captains of erudition, he put intellectual coin in our pockets.

No man more conservative (as all must be who hope to save for the future the best of the past). Preserving his ties to church, university, and political state, he stayed in partly from "a steady faith in the importance of continuity." Skepticism fuelled this faith, a perception that the evils of institutions, part and parcel of the nature of the beast, weren't "to be abolished by substituting a new set of institutions." But he wrote himself a socialist, more exactly "an orthodoxly-religious-politically-socialist man." Elitist, at the same time an inveterate democrat, he set his face against the acquisitive society, like Hawthorne, the elder James, and John Brooks Wheelwright, heroes he celebrated, one of them a personal friend. This mixed bag was good company and he adds to its sum.

You can trace his line of descent from nineteenth-century Utopians like long-forgotten Fourier, who wanted to settle us in communistic "phalansteries," Bronson Alcott of Fruitlands, a socialist community, not Marxist, however, and Welsh Robert Owen who founded New Harmony in Indiana's green and pleasant land. Actuated by the same impulse as these benevolent reformers, he meant to establish the City of God on earth. Unlike them, he wasn't a behaviorist or cocksure environmentalist—too worldly wise for that—and hardly supposed that we could pull ourselves up by our bootstraps. Estimating the crack in the bowl, he understood how all last things lie outside the scope of reform. Over St. Peter's School the spirit of three "high rebels," Ruskin, Arnold, and Newman, hovered persistently. He said what they rebelled against was "progress."

Of his many books, the autobiography comes last, but it seems right to say that all the books are autobiographical, so many versions of an etymologist in touch with root or radical meanings. The life he finished in his retirement, cherished labor, waited years on publication, too bad but not surprising. Whatever he wrote, said Cambon, restates "an underlying dissent from the established values of his society." It paid him back with silence. Society likes its heroes, if not compromised exactly, then willing to compromise, an Honest Abe who is only moderately this, a moderately pious Jesus Christ. He doesn't oblige.

I still see him (drawing here on the recollection of friends), smallish, brisk, neat in tweeds, a man for attachments but warmly distant, an informal man but mannerly, not slipshod, never that. With the ease that transcends etiquette went an elegant bearing, but even in age a touch of boyishness enlivened his face. Good at listening, he heard you out, then said his own say with style, sensibility, and candor. Speaking, he put his head down, the dark bright eyes squinting with thought. But a mystic tropism drew up his handsome jaw, jutting higher and ever higher. Not a calculated performer, he didn't study his words for effect. On the other hand, he didn't open his shirt front.

Ligatures weren't for him and he leaped without preamble from abstruse speculation to whimsical absurdities. Booming laughter acknowledged the absurdities, partly at his own expense. Entering the classroom, he left preliminaries aside. Others introduced themselves, called the roll, looked at notes. Superior to notes or not having any, he drew a large watch from his pocket, laid it down on the desk, then, lighting a cigaret, got going "in medias res." Slight but tense on the podium, he hinted at latent energies, like a coiled spring. The spring was firmly under control, though.

Other views, withershins to this one, modify or amplify his image in the mind's eye. His teacher's job consumed him, and unselfconscious gyrations suggested to students that he lived on some higher plane, off by himself. He twitched, grimaced, shot his jaw up, putting his neck in peril, made sudden penetrations, tortured unlit cigarets into tiny shreds. What the students thought seemed important to this master who was also a student, and questions needing answers kept them on the boil. Talk in his classroom, never *bavard*, was always to the center, the sacred text he held in his hand.

"Apostle to the midwest," he called himself, a whimsical characterization. Well-meaning accounts, making much of the apostleship, have him converting the heathen. Would that it were so, but in the nature of things he failed to convert them. Not that Michigan was less tractable than anyplace, USA. Out there in the world, though, it was all savage Boeotia.

Dear Joe Lee Davis, the best of the department in Austin's later days, evokes him at The Bull Ring, 111 West Huron Street, the "aristodemocracy" he organized in Ann Arbor. Who will forget those heady times when Warner Rice and Kenneth Burke "argued together at the bar over foaming steins while goggle-eyed graduate students drank in every word." Etc. This vignette, more poetry than truth, has its charm. Years after, Burke, back in town for a visit, encountered a survivor from the good old days. Boring them to death as ever but unmarked by time, he kept watch before the portals of knowledge. His business and pleasure was denying you access. There before Austin came on the scene, he ushered him out at the end. Recognizing Professor X, their immemorial antagonist, Burke couldn't remember his name.

Austin, said his wife Toni, "had ever felt an 'exile' in the Middle West," but flaneurs on either coast aren't to take comfort from a putdown. The sojourner for truth stood on the outside, and wherever he parked his bags existed in the university as a kind of fifth column or living reproach. "I belong," he said, with those "whose lot it is to live 'on the boundary.'" This neither-here-nor-there place left him open to all weathers, and to the unthinking ardors of parochial men who live under one flag.

In the 1950s a severe nervous breakdown laid him low, perhaps it enriched him. "Relief and release and emancipation," he called it. The same "'vastation' of strength and pride" overtook James the Elder, either breakdown or conversion. "It may be," Austin said, "that one is not obliged to choose between the two." He inclined toward the latter, believing that purgation precedes illumination. It doesn't seem likely that he meant to cheer us up or cheer himself up, as when heartless poets affirm that the best is yet to be, and I think this painful caesura, opening in the middle years, illuminated for him the provisionality of everything he stood for.

Toward the end, his labors met stony soil. Strength and eyesight failed, and the man who lived for his writing, addressed to the greater world, wrote letters, addressed to a few. They show him "moody, introspective, and self-distrustful," gripped by "a bleak and black state of depression." His autobiography, now about to go off in the mails yet again, hasn't wowed them in the courts of erudition and commerce, and he wonders whether "I have 'shot my bolt,' have lost my usefulness."

Isolated in Providence, Rhode Island, a final way station, he regretted "that we live in such a barbarous age." He said it grew steadily worse. He wasn't an old man grousing and hadn't lost his taxonomer's eye. Bad ideas, long maturing, finally ripe, were the culprit. He lived to see the discrediting of his empirical faith, sapped by new theory, Platonizing and self-referential. Let us have no more of the Word made flesh, they said, inflamed by a hatred of *terra damnata*. Where there used to be a text was a pool for Narcissus.

No one, said an old friend, felt more touched by the approval of his fellows than he. It didn't crown his last days and this festered. However, he wrote: "We have to do our work, our 'thing,' *ohne Hast, ohne Rast*." Applause or its absence weren't in it.

From the beginning, he cared little for prizes, even wages. At St. Peter's, they never made a dime. That was all right with an eleemosynary man. "I want to seek those things which are, for me, their own rewards," he said in his thirties. Among the desired things, truth headed the list. He spent a lifetime pursuing it, though knowing a will-o-the-wisp when he saw one. Not the goal but the search itself kept him going, however, and if he was lucky offered sufficient reward.

# 11

## Francis Fergusson: The Critic as Janus

Some critics win us by their fierce single-mindedness, like Yvor Winters when he doesn't deject us. Francis Fergusson, by contrast, is an ecumenical critic who can't help seeing all round. Most have a purview, but his view is comprehensive. That isn't always fortunate, and perhaps his inclusive psychology denies the chance for sharp distinctions. Writing that has an ax to grind, for example satire, succeeds as it distinguishes. In Pope's model satires, you are never in danger of confusing good and bad, nor do these opposites interpenetrate, making judgment uneasy. A higher kind of art accommodates without judging, though. Coordinating endlessly, Shakespeare leaves subordination to others. If you want exclusive answers, you won't appeal to him. Fergusson is among the accommodators.

He wrote for fifty years, covering the spectrum from high energy (Dante) to low (Eugene O'Neill). But everything got his respectful attention, O'Neill included, and whatever the subject he detected a scruple of use. Generally a positive modifies his negative view, perhaps a mark of kindliness but we must thank his Scottish thriftiness as well. The Roman god Janus, who looked two ways at once, gives his likeness, vivid in essays and reviews beginning in the 1920s and coming down to the proximate past. A good way to make his acquaintance is to read in the anthology put together by George Core and John McCormick, *Sallies of the Mind* (1998). "Sallies" is felicitous, meaning energetic incursions.

Reflections on T. S. Eliot and his impersonal theory of art lead off the collection. Fergusson isn't an adulator, unlike his contemporary and friend R. P. Blackmur, and the Eliot he writes about has his warts on. Primarily, of course, Eliot is the emancipating critic who freed us from the shackles of belles lettres. Readers who read from more than an impulse to see their own likeness must be in his debt. Reading poetry, he said, we will want to read it "primarily as poetry and not another thing." Cultural historians value it for extrinsic reasons but Eliot insists that its value is intrinsic, never in the service of—. All this, Fergusson acknowledges.

But Eliot's impersonal theory goes further, suggesting that art is autonomous. Perhaps this proposition is less true than cautionary, meant to keep us out of the hands of Professor X. But its effect is to exclude, hence to diminish. Drawing a sanitary cordon around the poem, it ignores the many filaments that connect it to the poet and the world that contains them both. It seems needlessly pure of Eliot to do this, even testifying to a personal shrinking.

Taking issue with modern criticism's Great Cham, Fergusson nails the inadequacy of a criticism that fails to relate art and life. Ultra-fastidious Eliot resembles those French Symbolist poets who banked on "poésie pure" to free them from the trials of existence. Paul Valéry is one, "the high priest of pure poetry." Everybody's exemplary modern poet, Eliot's included, he keeps the wind between noisome life and himself. The other side of his intellectual rigor is a kind of solemn and sensational crudity when it comes to human relations. But Fergusson's target isn't the impersonal artist. On the contrary. Art that excludes human values is marred by "an inability to escape the personal." This is surprising, and a palpable hit.

Eliot's limitation doesn't explain away his poetry, though, for "it really is poetry, and measures up to those purely esthetic standards in the midst of which it was born." Weakness and strength go together in him, also—a big jump, and most never take it—in his critic. Knowing where he comes from, Fergusson knows how this may abridge what he sees. In an essay on the Humanists, moral mandarins like Irving Babbitt, he hears the note of personal nostalgia in their hostile reporter, Malcolm Cowley. It isn't really on the point when Cowley asks us what Humanism has to do with the scene outside his window: "with the jobless men who saunter in the dusk, or the dying village, or the paper mill abandoned across the river—this mill whose owners have gone south where labor is cheap." The critical position the question takes rise from, emotionally close to Fergusson's own, appeals decidedly to "human values," and their absence in Eliot is a reason to fault him. At the same time, Fergusson is aware that sentimentality taints the appeal, in Cowley, perhaps in himself.

Cowley, a great man and great man of letters, was primarily a social critic. But in matters that require fine calibrating, you don't want to be primarily anything. Keats's chameleon is an image for the artist, and Fergusson might be thinking of its litmus paper-like self in his sympathetic account of Jacques Maritain's "creative intuition." The fully fledged reader of poetry, he tells us, "must quiet the feelings, the senses, and the mind, lest his intuition vanish." But this attractive imperative carries with it a whiff of that chilliness he reprehends in Eliot, still more in Valéry, whose pure poetry is based on "the sad delectation of poetry's self love." Good to compose yourself, Fergusson thinks, but do that too completely and you're dead. The "circumambient" view or knack of having it both ways is this critic's hallmark, his fault, if that is the right word, also his virtue, and defines the civilized man.

The back-and-forth goes on, aggravating perception—increasing it, no doubt, but itching at us while it does this. The Janus-like critic resembles his version of Shakespeare, whose "sense of analogy is perhaps too productive, burgeoning too richly in all directions." That is a capital insight into Shakespeare's way of reading the world, and whether it is a fault or virtue isn't easy to say. His Henry V, according to a comic character, Fluellen, is like Alexander the Great. How is that? Both were born beside a river, "and there is salmons in both." This absurdity is very close to essential Shakespeare. Incorrigibly "irredentist," he annexes territories next to his own on the ground of resemblances nobody had spotted before him.

Something like his habit of linking things up or opening them up to the exasperation of compartmentalizing critics like Winters seems tenable of Fergusson's judgments. Just when you think he has got the matter settled, he looks at it again. In his multifaceted criticism, "Hills peep o'er hills, and Alps on Alps arise." His view of Ibsen has more perspective than anyone else's. Shaw saw a hero and Synge a newspaperman, while Fergusson makes room for both. In *The Idea of a Theater* (1949), his most famous book, he argues a similarity between "the form of the life" of *Ghosts* and Greek tragedy, handling Ibsen's play with the same considerateness that belongs

to *Oedipus the King*. But this is only his first take, and needs qualification.

Ghosts, listened to or looked at harder, lacks the verbal music of
Racine, the sophistication of Hamlet, and the scope of the
Sophoclean chorus. But "it has its own hidden poetry," expressed
as a movement of the psyche out of darkness into seeing. This reading is assimilated in another, though, or amplified by another, and
the violently clear surface of the play obscures its real life and underlying form. The theater Ibsen wrote for, too tidy for truth, sub-
verts his poetic vision. The vision is expansive, the theater "cabined,
cribbed, and confined." Doorknobs turn, teacups rattle in their saucers, absorbing reality in a merely verisimilar art. Paradoxically,
the more verisimilar, the less real. There isn't enough reality in Ibsen.

Fergusson's strictures, informed by the same psychology that
found something wanting in Eliot's impersonal theory, depend on
his sense of the world around the play. After all, art-in-a-vacuum is
heresy. Life impinges on art, and the cask must always smell of the
wine that steeped it first.

\*   \*   \*

Crippled by Parkinson's disease, Fergusson stopped writing well
before his death in 1986. How many still read him at the end is a
question. Austin Warren, dead the same year and fallen from favor,
is a similar case. Up-to-date publishers no longer published either.
Both wrote luminous criticism, Fergusson's going back to *Hound
& Horn* days. I once owned his copies of that magazine, its last
issue appearing a half-century before he died. One of his poems,
"Suite for Winter," seems to remember his death in the week before
Christmas, "when the year moves toward cold and dark."

The vapid time he grew old in cared more for talking heads than
his American brand of *gravitas*, like a very intelligent cowboy's.
He didn't raise his voice or kick against the pricks. People like
Ibsen's (viewed through Fergusson's eyes), their ardent explicit-
ness offering "not a shred of manners to clothe their scruples in,"
were no kin of his. Though a professed atheist, he warmed to Dante
the pilgrim, who wins through, like certain heroes of Shakespeare's,
as he reaches "an innocence of total obedience to the will of God."
That isn't an idea for "the fashion of these times," Shakespeare's

phrase in *As You Like It* where the times are weighed and found wanting. They lack humility, and Fergusson, espousing it, stands on the outside.

Whatever his politics, he was through-and-through conservative, meaning that he conserved the best of the past as the only guarantee of the future. His window on the world was classical, corrected by medieval and Shakespearean apprehensions. But "classical," meaning Greek and Latin, means other things too, requiring that we look at people against their background, not in splendid isolation. "I am myself alone," says Shakespeare's Richard III, a romantic hero-villain. His direction is to the ego, Fergusson's is outward and social. It isn't accidental that his best-known criticism is dramatic.

He saw life as the fruitful repetition of an unchanging pattern. We are born, come to our height, and die, refreshed along the way by goodness and distracted by the problem of evil. Like Jacques Maritain, a notable presence in Princeton during Fergusson's years, he cultivated knowledge, less for *praxis*, as older critics might have put it, but for *gnosis*: not to change the world but to see into its essence. Maritain, remembering Bacon's famous apothegm, "Knowledge is power," said something like: The object of knowledge is not power; the object of knowledge is truth. The colleges and universities Fergusson taught in have moved on since his day, and their reading of knowledge gives priority to social engineering. He cared about change-for-the-better and cared deeply for knowledge. But unlike the president of Princeton in his/ her latest incarnation, he understood that the two aren't sequential. Neither does the second come out of the first.

His criticism of modern fiction is like a palimpsest, and the older or classical understanding of the world is still visible under present-day versions. Reviewing three sociopolitical novels, James Gould Cozzens' *Guard of Honor*, Robert Penn Warren's *All the King's Men*, and Lionel Trilling's *Middle of the Journey*, he invoked *The Iliad*, saying how Homer, diagnosing disaster, "does not prescribe a cure." He doesn't pull a long face, either. Trilling, a novelist of ideas, might have taken this to heart. If only he had smiled a little, as Shaw did toward the end, "when he suddenly sensed his fifty years of brisk intellectual conversation as a farce against a dark and mysterious background." But though respectful of the mystery and unwilling to pronounce, Fergusson wasn't open-minded. The critical relativist is that, emptied out of criteria. His only canon is the absence of canons. Fergusson moves toward conclusions.

Like Austin Warren, he was essentially a comparativist. His special passions were the theater, Dante, and Shakespeare. Necessarily, he read Dante in Italian. The Thomistic philosophy that organized the *Commedia* engaged him, but less than the up-front poem. If you meant to deal with the poem, you had to use the very words it was couched in. He belonged to the academy, in company with many modern American intellectuals, but lived in it uneasily for the sake of a living, never of it. Academics, dazzled by ideas and mindful of language only as it carries them, shuck the husk and go straight for the kernel. He wanted to know what the hurry was.

In an essay comparing Dante in the *Purgatorio* with Shakespeare in *The Tempest*, he elucidates his authors' relation to religious belief. Putting on his scholar's hat, he shows how Shakespeare's art and Dante's were fed by religion. The abiding thing for each of them wasn't God, however, "but action, or love, the ceaseless movement of the human spirit." The love is the thing to focus on, not of the world over yonder but this one. "I am one who, when love breathes in me, take note," Dante tells a rival poet. The description holds for Fergusson, and suggests what prompted his writing.

Like Henry James, he feared abstractions and said you couldn't have an "art-in-general." James, in his core a dramatist, insisted on presenting rather than explaining. In *The Golden Bowl*, for instance, "a drama without a stage and an ethical debate without abstract concepts." His notorious verbosity, endlessly elaborating minutiae, derived from this insistence. That was what happened when you assimilated novels to plays, creating both the play and the theater it plays in. Most critics of James think the man who talked too much was indulging his bent for abstraction. Fergusson, looking deeper, got it right.

He had a natural philosopher's eye, eyes close to the ground, not far-seeing like his friend Robert Oppenheimer's. Convention associates the empirical habit with the scientific intelligence, but Oppenheimer, looking down his hawk's nose, dismissed it. "The one thing the scientist does not want to do is count," he said in conversation. Fergusson, less cavalier, no sweeping cape or imperial gesturing for him, was prone to checking things out. He wasn't a brute naturalist, however, and the figure in the carpet absorbed him. Characterizing Dante, he drew his own portrait, "as scrupulous as a modern scientist," the kind Oppenheimer disparaged.

The results he came up with were offered not as final truth but as a working hypothesis. Like another lifelong friend, R. P. Blackmur, who called criticism the formal discourse of an amateur, he read and wrote in a provisional spirit. His insights are "suggestions for the reader of good will to mull over." But he is hardly an "on the one hand and then on the other hand" kind of critic, and his inquiring stance mustn't be confused with irresolution. Nothing easier than to make up your mind, provided there isn't much on it. Like Hamlet, whose agonized thinking becomes him, he locates himself in a country of half-lights between the extremes of the clarity most of us opt for. Paradoxically, this is where things look most nearly like themselves.

Some of his writing seems bread-and-butter work, like the piece on the Humanists, most of them forgotten, and some of it is only intelligent, as when he looks at Oedipus, the play and the complex. His long essay on *Hamlet* is more expository than one reader would wish, the flip side of a good man's modesty. Allen Tate called his two books on Dante "expository masterpieces," and praised him for pursuing "the point to be made rather than the argument to be exhibited." Show-offs do the latter, exhibiting themselves. A handful have something in them worth exhibiting, though, like Oscar Wilde, better in his prose than his person. Fergusson turns this relation around. Much superior to Wilde the man, he lacks his saving arrogance. Willing to teach us, he leaves the obiter dicta to others.

Like Tate, execrated in Princeton for his scandalous talk to their English Club on "Miss Emily and the Bibliographer," he fluttered the academic dovecotes. Miss Emily is Faulkner's heroine who murdered her lover and slept with his corpse, and the Bibliographer, a.k.a. the Professor of English, excelled, according to Tate, in laying out the corpus of literature. But the academic world is seductive, and Fergusson like Tate took color from it. (Austin Warren did too.) His prose is more unbuttoned than that of the superior critical intelligences he shares the time with: T. S. Eliot, Blackmur, Borges, Valéry. Great panjandrums in criticism, they would have no such readers as they could teach. For their criticism, that works out to a good. You don't catch them lapsing into casual chat, like this of Fergusson's: "I realize that it would be impossible to discuss the importance" of Dante, etc. "The topic would be too vast.... So I decided to interpret my assignment in a different way." Discharging the assignment, he is an enabler in criticism, not a competitor or would-be peer of the writers he criticizes, not a modern Oscar, the Critic as Artist.

What raises him from the ruck of the merely intelligent, like Virginia Woolf's Professor Raleigh, is his anti-reductive bias. Unlike his version of Polonius, who speaks in blank verse but suggests the heroic couplet, he doesn't impose on you by rhetoric rather than thought. The rhetorician boils things down or enlarges them, casting his truth in relief. That is the function of his neat antitheses and studied complementarities. Either way, the clarity he achieves is factitious, at any rate partial. Fergusson's art of criticism is "polysemous" (like the four-fold allegory of the Middle Ages), and he reads his texts under that rubric. An enchantress in the *Commedia*, though morally repugnant, retains some sort of being in her own right, aloof from moral judgment. She appears in different guises, but in all of them, he says, "we never lose the sense that she was somehow *there*, and her power and mystery remain when we leave her."

The residual thing is a way of distinguishing greater from lesser art. In the *Hamlet* essay, Fergusson compares Shakespeare and Euripides, a flashy satirist, brilliant but circumscribed, who aims for the center and hits it. Fergusson's direction, like Shakespeare's, is centrifugal. Going in the centripetal direction allows of epigrams and QED demonstrations, hardly negligible but taking in less territory. Irredentists want more. The literal meaning of *Hamlet*'s play-within-the-play is the fact of the crime, "but the trope and the anagoge"—medieval terms, lifted from Dante—put before us all mankind, weak, guilty, and foolish. The good man's temperament, patient even to a fault, lets this critic see things his brisker contemporaries pass over.

\* \* \*

In the late forties, Oppenheimer brought him to the Institute for Advanced Study in Princeton. A tight little community that looked to itself, it attracted more brains per square foot than any other place in the country. Einstein was only *primus inter pares*, his colleagues including Ernest Wigner, Oskar Morgenstern, and John Archibald Wheeler. Walking along Battle Road talking abstractedly into his dictaphone, Wheeler was the conceptualizing scientist to the life. Next door to him lived Erwin Panofsky, prince of iconographers, and his sons Wolfgang and Hans. They were the smart Panofsky and the dumb Panofsky, finishing first and second in the same Princeton class.

When Hermann Weyl elaborated his idea of symmetry, he had the ear of the man Blackmur called "Johnny" von Neumann. One summoned mathematics to the aid of esthetics, the other created games theory. And so on. Egos were outsize in this enclosed garden. R. P. Blackmur had a big one, Allen Tate and Roger Sessions running him a close second. At the Institute, Fergusson began the lecture series that turned into the Gauss Seminars in Literary Criticism, under Blackmur's direction. Comparison between them, friends of long standing, suggests what Fergusson was and wasn't.

Some seminars were better than good, but best was the shank of the evening, high thought and high living. In this context, Blackmur shone. Like an oracle at Delphi, he quoted Montaigne, Pascal, and "the poor verses of Venantius Fortunatus." (If you hadn't heard of Venantius, that was partly the point.) His head was in the clouds, the ones that circle Mount Olympus, and his learning staggered all who got within earshot. Some of it, the hole-in-corner bits, he cribbed from Saintsbury, needing to impress men less learned than him. His autodidact's education made him self-conscious, and Fergusson was the superior scholar. This is apparent in his critical prose, no stunting and nothing to prove.

Blackmur has more élan, Fergusson more assurance. His learning is the tip of the iceberg's, Blackmur's on the surface, though scarcely superficial. Sometimes he routed friends with a splendid, improbable apercu, Fergusson meanwhile keeping the even tenor of his way. You see this especially when they cope with foreign languages, like Dante's, a passion for both. French and German, novels, poems, and plays, were part of their stock-in-trade, even Russian. Expounding on "The Brothers K," Blackmur recited a litany. "Misha's socks had holes in them."

Writing on Stanislavsky and the Moscow Art Theater, Fergusson acknowledges that he has no Russian. Blackmur, our best American critic, couldn't help faking it in three or four different tongues. The way he pretended, as if he were the Stagyrite! But his clay feet were always showing. This had its charm. Once he commended a wine bar in Berlin, Kampenski's on the Kudamm. "Near the AmZoo," he said, "AmZoo" meaning "Near the Zoo." The charm wasn't obvious to everyone, and Frank Kermode, a straightforward critic without pretension, admired Fergusson but not Blackmur. He said he didn't "get" Blackmur, a generous admission. The thing Kermode missed, beyond correctness or good sense, was worth getting.

Fergusson had other things, enough to sustain the comparison between them. Uncommonly a nice man, he had as much spleen as nice John Crowe Ransom when he skewered Edna Millay. He knew what he liked and whereof he spoke, and his attack on Eugene O'Neill's "disheartening matrix of psychology, bathos, and cheap symbolism" is as good in the going-for-the-jugular kind as it gets. His vitriol isn't that exclusively, however, and the critic as Janus can't help relating O'Neill's helpless bombast to what looks like a plus. "Histrionic sincerity," Fergusson calls this positive side, but what kind of sincerity is that? It is of "the essence of mummery," Fergusson answers, giving and taking in the same breath. His attack, fortified with, not diluted by, appreciation, does justice to the mangler of words who nonetheless could "tent" us to the quick in *Long Day's Journey into Night*. You can't ask more of criticism than this.

Blackmur near the end soared into the stratosphere, but Fergusson stayed earthbound. A third figure on the Princeton scene, Stringfellow Barr called Winkie, reflects light on them both. Known to the press as a famous "educator," the co-founder of St. John's College, Annapolis, Barr lived on easy terms with fame; Blackmur doted on it; Fergusson ignored it. Like his unpretentious friend Winkie, he had a low ratio of side to his substance. Like his Dante, he was incorrigibly ad hoc, always "trying to authenticate his verses by making them obey only the particular voice." It didn't have to be "verses," and whatever the medium, the intonation was recognizably his.

He comes close to saying that in Dante, perhaps in art as a kind, the concrete transcends the universal. He belonged to no school but resembles the New Critics in harking back to small beer. In common with Dante, and the best critics in any generation, he understood that you don't participate in the heavenly vision by seeing life steadily and seeing it whole. The famous phrase, quoted in his essay on "The *Divine Comedy* as a Bridge across Time," is only rhetoric. Ignore its glozing counsels, Fergusson says, and concentrate on one strictly limited aspect of experience. That is how you build a bridge across time.

# 12

## Lucky Jim as I Remember Him

Kingsley Amis's death at seventy-three leaves me with old images and the need to sort through them. His talent, though not huge, was real, and like that Renaissance pope who warmed to the Papacy, he had the wit to enjoy what God gave him. An ego with a callus on it went with his endowment. Scanning the obits, he used to point with satisfaction to the chaps who hadn't made it to forty. If I was lucky, I might live as long as him. He was closing in on forty when he said this, and getting to that great age was the last thing on my mind.

In a photo taken near the end, he strikes an attitude outside his London club, the Garrick, round the corner from Trafalgar Square. His jaw juts and his belly is lined with good capon. Eyeglasses swing carelessly in his right hand, his eyes squinting fiercely at the camera. *Nemo me impune lacesset.* That isn't how I remember him, though.

We met at Princeton in the Fifties when Richard Blackmur brought him over for the Gauss Seminars. Talent spotter extraordinary, Blackmur had other finds, Al Alvarez, Jack Aldridge, Chomsky, Philip Roth, but none grabbed at life the way he did. At the Seminars, held Friday nights in Firestone Library, first names and nicknames were favored. Invited guests spoke knowingly of Ezra, Wystan, and Tom. Cal was Robert Lowell. Arch humor evoked titters, and Harry Levin, talking of Stendhal, wondered if you could see the Alps from Parma. In the front row, Hannah Arendt, not *gemütlich*, got to the heart of the matter. Kingsley sat in the back row, muttering under his voice, "Bloody Oxford!"

Later we joined forces in Rome and London, Swansea in Wales, Peterhouse College, Cambridge, one of his wrong turnings. Misery loves company, and we bucked each other up in Nashville, Tennessee, where I was dying with my boots on as chairman of Vanderbilt's English Department. One summer holiday—I don't remember where, even what country—we played on the beach and splashed in shallow water, mugging for the camera. I still have the film, Kingsley making his Sex-Life-in-Ancient-Rome face, Hilly in the background, tinder that needed chafing.

In the memoir he wrote in his last years, he went back in mind to Hilly and their early time together. Harmless and defenseless, he said she was. If things went wrong, it was probably her fault, anyway she thought so. "Smashing" in person, she mocked her good looks, "eyes like Garbo's but a mouth like Donald Duck's." Long afterwards, remarried to a classical scholar, she found herself in Ann Arbor, Michigan. Opening a fish-and-chips shop, she called it "Lucky Jim's."

After seventeen years, Kingsley moved in with Jane Howard. Taller than most but not stooping like some whose height makes them self-conscious, she descended from the Howards he read about in school. Jane had been around famous men, like Arthur Koestler, from her youth, marrying one or two of them. But writing was her pole star, and her novel, *After Julius*, I thought better than any of Kingsley's. Walking from the tube stop to their flat in Hampstead, you smelled coal smoke on the air in winter, mingled with the smell of Woodbines, the poor man's cigaret. All of us smoked it in those days.

As he got older, Kingsley tacked and trimmed, as which of us doesn't, but despite what you read, didn't change much. No whisk of the cape replaced the Angry Young Man with the Old Boy. At first a left-wing socialist, even a communist, according to his son Martin, he stood with Nye Bevan against the party elders. Quarreling with the elders got his juices flowing, and though his politics shifted rightwards, his instinct for combat never wobbled or dulled. An early target was Amis Senior, retired from clerking and a twice-shy observer in the Princeton house they rented from the Murray Kemptons. When the old man died, others took his place, Senator Fulbright, Sir John Gielgud, Anthony Armstrong-Jones.

Though blacks and Asians were non grata to Britain's "yabboes" on the right—this word of Kingsley's meaning rednecks, wherever found—he turned a blind eye on color. Like any genuine writer, in his deepest place he was a career-to-the-talents man. Causes didn't engage him. Princeton had its black community, manumitted slaves left over from antebellum times, but as remote as an article in the *National Geographic*. Nashville, however, had a fix on color and wouldn't let him ignore it. He was Chinese Gordon, surrounded by fuzzy-wuzzies, all of them white.

His observations, recorded in the memoir, fluttered their dovecote in Nashville. This wasn't Yoknapatawpha County, said one former colleague, shaking his head "more in sorrow than anger." He theorized that well-intentioned locals had played to Kingsley's conservative bias, wanting him to feel right at home. "Piling on copious racism," they became stage-Southerners, not understanding, poor dears, that color prejudice wasn't his thing. Another colleague traced his pique to wounded vanity, Kingsley's views on Vietnam, pro-U. S. all the way, having cost him the good will of Nashville's intelligentsia. Widely known on their own view for liberal feeling, they shut their doors against him.

Eager for news of the outside world, if only in a bottle, Kingsley made sure the *Daily Telegram* followed him over the water. When he fetched it from the mailbox, he was one of Maugham's nabobs, picking up his copy of the *Penang Times*. He put his experience of Penang, etc. into a novel, part of it set in rural Tennessee. The setting posed a problem, though, how to render Southern dialect, nearly the death of *Gone with the Wind*. Meeting the problem head on, then ignoring it completely, he shows you his special talent, invention.

The first time round, his astonished Englishman hears an irate local say: "Armageddon pierced staff. Arcane standard Hannah More." This translates to: "I'm gettin' pissed off. Ah cain't stand it any mo'." After that, spooning in the grits and hominy were the reader's business. Sometimes, however, Kingsley relaxed his rule. In the memoir, a colleague's wife asks him about the movie "Surr Laurence Oh-livyay made of *Oh-thello*." "They made him look like a black mayun!" she says indignantly. He "toked, even woked" that way too.

Jane was with him in Nashville, and later, in the London papers, reported on the land of cotton. Rev. King had just been murdered, and she thought she knew why. Yabboes were the most of them below Mason-Dixon, only Hal, my graduate student, getting her affectionate notice. John Birchers in Vanderbilt's English Department perked up their ears. Naming this friend, she handed them a hostage, and they kicked him out of the program.

A portrait in the living room of the rented house near campus the Amises lived in remembered the landlady, wife of an absent colleague. She looked like Beulah Bondi, everybody's Mom in old Hollywood movies. You knew the simpering smile concealed a heart of stone. The year before, I had hired the first Jew since man knoweth not to join the University's English Department, and Missus sat beside me at the welcoming dinner. Looking down the table, she looked at him skeptically. "He's rather—urban," she said.

Beneath the picture on the wall, Kingsley and Jane shared a writing surface, chuckling over their work. "Good, isn't it?" said he, rattling off a sentence. "Jolly good," she told him. He was "Kingers," sometimes "Bunny." Shrouding her own talent, she asked you to pay attention to his. He would have been happy with bangers and mash but she served him Cornish game hen and aubergine with stuffed tomatoes. On cold nights he wore a stocking cap, work of her hands.

She had a gift, not a taste, for religious experience, and her moist Io's eyes appealed for understanding. If you gave it, she cranked the portcullis up, letting you into the castle. On her grande dame side, she froze impertinence, though. When a friend of my daughter's presumed on their mutual acquaintance, she did his business like a chilly Brit in a Noel Coward play. "Ah, yes, Karen," she said. "How nice. Do give her our love. Good bye."

She and my then wife, called Phil, made a pair like the short and tall heroines in Shakespeare's dream play, one "low and little," the other a "painted maypole." Watching them in the kitchen, Kingsley thought of Mutt and Jeff. For a New Year's Eve bash in Nashville, the two created a Lucullan feast, starting off with a country pate. "I sure like your meat loaf," said one of the guests. Kingsley's second marriage ended in divorce like his first, only sooner. But he could never be alone, and Jane having left him, he moved back in with Hilly and her third husband. By then, he said, all of us were old.

\*\*\*

A professional who never stopped writing, he never surpassed his first novel, *Lucky Jim*. Saying so, I don't diminish it or him. I mean that the novel was once-and-for-all, like *Chrome Yellow* and *Antic Hay*, a classic the day it fell from the press. I had it open when Alexander, child of my right hand, was born. Reading through the wee hours outside Princeton Hospital's delivery room, I forgot the Sturm and Drang on the other side of the wall. That says little for my character but much for Kingsley's novel. One of Shakespeare's heroes, logging time in the hospital, is told to leave them laughing, not easy. *Lucky Jim*—you remember when you read it, like Pearl Harbor and the death of FDR—is able to do that.

Read it twice and the seams show. A second-class sensibility, like Woody Allen's, stitches the jokes together. Nuance you mustn't look for, and the feeling-good story would make Dickens blush. A poet-friend of Kingsley's, judging his second novel, almost up to his first, gives its flavor. Like a second helping of raspberries, he says. But the jokes are funnier than a punch in the nose.

E.g., when Dixon, the Amis character, having nudged an archery butt left over from Merrie England, makes his "crazy-peasant face," or a persistent student reduces him to his Eskimo face, neck abolished by sucking it down between his shoulders, face shortened and broadened by half. Hoping to escape detection, he doesn't. Cyril Connolly, an Establishment figure in Kingsley's youth, heard at a party that these faces were worth seeing. "Would you mind just—?" he asked, in that elliptical way of theirs, leaving the rest of the question to you. Not wanting to show off but wanting to oblige, Kingsley performed as requested. "I don't think that's funny," Cyril Connolly said.

Some of the humor acts out aggression. Kingsley had plenty, and it seems a good thing that his talent went to laughs. Like him, the Amis hero is filled with impotent fury, and bunching his fists, thrusts his hands in his pockets. He hated Toby jugs, all that whimsy under the squashed fedora. He hated his Professor's cat, symbol of domesticity. "Scratch 'em," he told it, "pee on the carpets." Most of all, he hated the academic world and the thin gruel it said was nutritious. Teachers like Prof. Welch, cunning under the obtuseness, practiced a sort of "stingy, stodgy caution." This extended to the classroom, a Gobi Desert of the mind, and the guests they had over for dinner. No beakers full of the warm South, and the coffee was sure to be Instant.

Academics, keeping abreast, read the *Times Literary Supplement* (*TLS*), Kingsley opting for *The News of the World*. Hot stuff, like the sleaze at the checkout counter in American supermarkets, it gave him something to do Sundays before the pubs opened. Eyes glued to the page, like a mad scholar in the British Museum, he hunted scenarios. "Police officers stated that Fortescue, emerging from the Underground, fell at the feet of the woman and committed his offense."

He had a few truths inscribed in his phylactery, among them that nice things were nicer than nasty ones. The things included girls, strong drink, and music with a tune in it. Though the ideological pals of his youth said "fascist" America would freeze his blood, he loved it from day one, "my second country," incurring the hatred of all middle-class hating lefties. He liked American names, not homogeneous and not going back to the Conquest, Bugsy Siegel, Joe Montana, Muhammad Ali. American glitz spoke to something childlike in him. He was Christopher Newman, taking it all in on the first day of Creation.

His addiction to low-frequency words was part of this. I remember "jejeune," having been scolded when I didn't get it right. Proper speech, meant to put you in your place, was verboten, however. "It's me," he said emphatically, not "I." But America's slovenly way with words got his goat. Often touchy, never "aggravated," he would show you the door if you advertised "disinterest" when all you were was bored.

His insistence on getting things straight verged on pedantry, setting his rational side against the provincial one. (On his provincial side, he knew what he liked.) A Thoreauvian who would have hated Thoreau, he cut his own hair and spoke bitterly of tweed jackets with leather patches on the elbows. But his contempt for embellishment didn't extend to the houses he lived in. Living in Cambridge, he had a cricket pitch out back. The Fellows picked on him at Cambridge, dropping a dead mouse in his inkwell, but he knew how to handle this, and invited an ex-Army chum, smelly and raggedy, to one of their black tie and wing collar "feasts." Trying on roles, he played country squire in his Georgian house at Barnet, terminus of London's Northern Line. Outside, on Hadley Common, Shakespeare's characters fought each other in the Wars of the Roses. But he was a sojourner right to the last, and bivouacked in most of the houses.

An aristocratic glaze overlaid his plebeian one. Richard Blackmur, a snob (among other things), bristled if you took liberties, answering "*Arrivederla*" to your informal "*Arrivederci*." Where did he get off, Kingsley wanted to know, all that high-and-mighty? He himself did a good imitation of the great panjandrum, though, clipped, a little distant, British to his fingertips. Before anybody thought of dubbing him Sir Kingsley, he was the lord of the manor.

This loose liver in his salad days looked at life from a moralist's perspective. The French saying, to understand all is to forgive all, was the Devil's saying, and he dragged us back a second time to Clint Eastwood's modern morality play, *Dirty Harry*. Its psychopathic villain evoked no sympathy from him. When the villain gets his, he cheered wildly, eliciting stares. "Politically correct" was a flag to his bull, and putting his head down, he gored the mincers of words. "*Saeve indignatio*," he might have written over his lintel.

But the comparison with Swift, ventured by others, won't work unless it notices the ugly side, mounting to crazy. Just try telling him he might be wrong. Having made up his mind, he let you know what was on it. He did this with gusto, steaming into battle with the colors flying, Britannia's, before the Empire went to the dogs. The brutality of his critical prose makes you blink. Dismissing Keats or Jane Austen, he wasn't downright, only coarse. Skewering convention was his fatal chimera: "rotten Italy," "filthy French food." After a while, it gets old.

He was good on French waiters, not cut out for the job, he said, because the power that went with it encouraged them to look down their noses. Unluckily, however, this led to reflections on Frenchness, something you didn't want to go in for. The man who loved women didn't get them all wrong, only mostly. Among his models was Henry Fielding, "the only non-contemporary worth reading." This novelist, though funny, wasn't much of a thinker. He had kind words for boorish Squire Weston (in *Tom Jones*), while ridiculing his bluestocking sister. Unbecoming in a female, she exercised her mind. "How enviable to live in the world of his novels," says an Amis hero. Duty was plain then, evil rose from malevolence, and moral seriousness didn't require "evangelical puffing and blowing."

Apologists will tell you that Kingsley the idol smasher isn't really out to demolish old favorites but has a satirist's eye for their sheeplike idolaters. For example Col. Blimp, who despised the modern world but exalted the Middle Ages when everyone knew his place. Lord David Cecil, whose idiot-savant face Kingsley liked putting on, worshiped "filthy Mozart." And so forth. Sometimes, however, whatever the voice, "the hands are the hands of Esau." Like splenetic John Updike, making Harry Angstrom bear the weight of his spleen, the Angry Old Man has his stalking horses. If you believe him, that "sexist-chauvinist pig" in the novels isn't him. A lot of the time, it is, though.

Walking round his library, you get to know him better. Early on, he read the novelist Anthony Powell, whose minimalist view of life, looking up from down under, he found "utterly congenial." His favorite poets were Housman and Kipling, just below them Philip Larkin, product of the same red-brick-of-the-mind as himself. Housman and Larkin wrote a few poems that belong to us all; Kipling is a genius, as good almost as the best. Kingsley valued them partly for what they weren't, though. They weren't Modernist. A type of the modern man, he detested Modernism, not some of it, all of it, and knew where the movement was headed. Doom awaited "the fools and charlatans" who assisted at its birth. Naming names, he cited Pound and Picasso. Times to come may conclude that he was right about Picasso, and already it seems clear that Pound is two-thirds fudge. But about the other third, Kingsley was clueless.

Chucking the academic life after his stint at Cambridge, he kept the ferrule for old times' sake. He was born to teach, not unqualified praise. The part he liked best was when you handed out grades. Edmund Blunden, untouched by Modernism, got a high pass. So did John Betjeman. Of course he made nothing of Donne.

His biographer had to know that John D. MacDonald was "by any standards" a better writer than Saul Bellow. Another crony recorded his opinion of Bach: "Johann Sebastian is all right, but I prefer Johann Christian." Maybe *de gustibus* doesn't cover this preference. Kitsch tickled his funny bone, not least because the cognoscenti despised it. One of the Andrews Sisters, the high-voiced one, Maxene, died the same day he did. Everybody old enough remembers how the three of them made life less gloomy in wartime. Had he hung on a little longer, I imagine him tipping his hat to Maxene. "Better than bloody Bartok," something like that.

We shared a passionate commitment to American jazz, but quarreled over its essentials, like Greek Orthodox priests. When making the blessing, do you hold up two fingers or three? Raised on the British cornetist Humphrey Lyttleton—he played the Hippodrome in Golders Green, north of Hampstead—Kingsley thought this music should swing. The Chicago variety, mostly white man's jazz, did that, drowning out his personal demons. Among clarinetists, Pee Wee Russell, strictly Chicago, made him happy, but hearing George Lewis he cringed. Authentic New Orleans, this often mournful black man provoked night thoughts. Once when I put on a platter at my house, Kingsley rose and clicked off the machine.

Menace stalked the corners of his world like dragons in old maps, marking Terra Incognita. Under a colleague's laugh, he heard peals of horrid mirth, echoing from old films about murders in castles. Motorcars spooked him. One noses into the garage and "with a single frightful bound," stops only short of the wall, another lows obscenely when the motor wakes it to shuddering life. At the thought of travel, he made his stabbed-in-the-back face. "I Like It Here," he said, refusing to budge unless forced to his feet like a camel.

He didn't drive, or wouldn't, and in a world where you don't exist except for the cards in your wallet, didn't have a license. He had been behind the wheel when someone got injured or killed. He wouldn't fly. Coming to Nashville from London, he crossed the ocean by boat and did the overland journey by train. Cook's Ltd. kept pace with him each step of the way. Even in youth, he was a valetudinarian Kingsley, surviving from Victorian times.

I don't know that he had a drinking "problem." He drank a lot. Early days in Swansea, we opened the pubs together, and finished lunch in Princeton with a tot of Green Chartreuse. At the movies in Nashville, *Bonnie and Clyde*, a matinee performance, he sucked on a pocket flask of bourbon. He was easy with his liquor, never drunk, often elevated. In a world of his own, he dared you to climb up there with him.

When he traveled to Rome, he brought his shrink along, the way Byron brought a pet *gondoliere* to Pisa. Entraining for London in the middle of the night, he had to leave from that tucked-away little station out beyond San Lorenzo's. We got him to the station but he wouldn't let go of my arm. Philip Larkin had found him a recording for the ages, on clarinet the "tattered majesty" of old Johnny

Dodds, on trumpet young Charlie Shavers. I could have a tape if I promised not to leave until the train pulled away from the platform. After he was seated, he peered from the window, gesticulating frantically like a stage Italian. Stay put, his hands were telling us, and we had to.

Though he dreaded Abroad, he turned uneasiness to haughtiness. Pausing by the tables in front of Trastevere's Cafe Noiantro, he took in the scene, then adjusted his Evelyn Waugh mask. "Lots of wogs," he said. Somebody had squelched him when he was young, not any more. At the Garden House Hotel on the Backs in Cambridge, the stuffy patrons and stuffier waiters looked with horror at his open-necked shirt. Wearing a boiled shirt, the sommelier showed him the wine list, murmuring a benediction in French. "I'll have the Graves," Kingsley told him, pronounced to rhyme with "waves." Lifting his glass, he sniffed, tasted, and spat the wine on the table. "Very good," he said.

Watching him with her children, Betty Fussell thought they adored him, knowing him for one of their own. His fears were theirs, kept at bay through rituals, words in daytime, at night the laughter in the dark. The bad bits remembered from childhood still festered, but he milked them for comedy, some of it doubtful. English Sundays made his thumbs prick, and he might have panicked that Sunday in Regent's Park, dense with post-prandial strollers. He made sure they gave him room, though. Commandeering a pram left outside the public toilet, he rolled along the walkways, eyes starting, spastic fingers clutching at air.

Paul Fussell, one of his biographers, said that what was missing in his early time was joy. Getting older, he made up for this, using sex like a soak in the hot tub. Larkin has a poem about the year the Beatles got started, bringing free-and-easy sex along with them. "1963. Just too late for me." It wasn't too late for Kingsley.

Putting it mildly, he liked women's breasts. "She had the biggest pair of knockers I had ever seen in the flesh and still unequaled. When you stood at an ordinary conversational distance from her, you found you were standing too close." But flat-chested women had their points. "I could love her and her," he said, quoting his least favorite poet. "I could love any."

His approach to sex mixed energy, eternal hopefulness, and coldness. Much ahead of his time, he understood that the age of candies, flowers, and dilly-dallying was past. If you propositioned many, he thought, you were likely to score with a few. Mowing them down, he wasn't acting out neuroses but having fun, like Don Juan before the blahs overtook him. The time he tried to hustle my wife into bed, I made a scene in Technicolor, almost the end of our friendship. "Nothing personal, old man," he said.

\*  \*  \*

Physically, he bore the stigma of his class. Before the National Health, everybody like him grew up with bad teeth. People higher on the totem pole, better off or knowing better, went to the dentist. If you were among them, you voted three times, one vote for your townhouse, probably in South Kensington, another for your cottage in the Home Counties, a third for your college, Oxbridge, it went without saying. This privilege bred attitudes.

I remember smoking in the entracte at Covent Garden Opera with my friend Paul, uncommonly bright but out of pocket and wearing ratty sneakers called "plimsols." Behind him and facing me, a florid-faced Englishman—he wore the uniform they favored then, black suit and pale-colored shirt with French cuffs and detachable white collar—looked us over cap-a-pie, beginning with the sneakers. I still see the contempt in his eyes.

Kingsley challenged all that and the world that produced it. Once, at a wine pub in Fleet Street, El Vino's, we sat with Henry Fairlie, a public personality whose reputation has ebbed. Sneering at "our cousins over the sea," he asked with mock-sincerity, "Pray, what do you Americans have to teach us?" Getting in before me, Kingsley leaned forward. "Courtesy," he said.

His gallantry was Dickensian, and Dickens was the English novelist he is closest to, both the warmhearted man and the wrongheaded one. Each of these writers had a supersensitive ear, attuned to uncanny vibrations. With this went a talent for spotting resemblances not apparent to anyone else. The two together are key to his art of mimicry. More than simple imitation, it involves the creation of a new species. Like Dickens's Major Bagstock in *Dombey and Son*, he brought forth his repertory of memorable types, as it might be Major Bagstock, friend of the Duke of York, Joey B. who wouldn't adulate, Joe the plain old soldier, Joseph, true to himself and an affront to others. The comprehensive man, playing many parts in one person, worked up his roles by looking in the mirror. He did best when he made a target to shoot at.

Partly sinister like Bazarov in Turgenev's *Fathers and Sons*, he was our bright side with its sliver of darkness. Old verities, including prohibitions, didn't faze him. This was appalling, fascinating too, like his sexual conquests, the source of envious nail biting. Some modern critics, stuffed with psychobabble, have him "overcompensating." He was what he seemed, though, a normally sexed young man who kicked over the traces. Conventional in his slant on things and as often as most of us "honest and kindly," words for Jim Dixon, he differed from his hero, being touched with genius.

The last time we met, he had moved back to London. Over drinks at his club, we talked about Rome and his hairbreadth escape under cover of darkness. This was matter for laughs. I remembered the jazz tape he'd promised to get me, the "tattered majesty" of my favorite clarinetist. But he was safely home and had forgotten all about it.

# 13

## James Dickey's Dear God of the Wildness of Poetry

Dickey's god of poetry is more Dionysus than Apollo. But that is a truism, i.e., not a sufficient truth, and his releasing is also controlling. Though he opened new fields for poetry, he did this partly to subdue them, breaking untilled ground to the plough. A poem of the sixties, "For the Last Wolverine," shows him on the wild side, but the poem and poems like it "rise beyond reason." Lesser poets are irrational, but he is himself and superior to easy generalization.

He liked poems about animals, the wilder the better. Doomed to extinction, the wolverine gnaws its prey and looks straight at eternity, dimly aware of being the last of its kind. The poet doesn't mind if the reader thinks of him. Omnivorous and insatiable, he is like Thoreau devouring the woodchuck, all of it, hooves, hair, and hide. He hopes to effect its total transmigration.

When he died at the beginning of 1997, he had dwindled, said his friend Lance Morrow, to a seventy-three year-old ruin, "his flesh slack over the armature of bone, the lungs and liver a disaster." *Life* magazine, introducing the pop icon thirty years before, didn't script an ending like this. The "bare-chested bard" it celebrated "looks, acts and often talks exactly like a professional football coach." Standing 6' 3" and weighing 205 lbs., he has a paunch and huge biceps, incidentally a fresh literary voice. The biceps, etc. get into the voice in an elegy "For the Death of Lombardi." This coach of the Green Bay Packers thought winning was the only thing. In the poem he is dying of cancer, and his boys, Hornung, Nitschke, and Kramer, storied names in Green Bay, stand around him. "We're with you," they say, having to believe there's such a thing as winning. "We're with you all the way/ You're going forever, Vince."

This sounds like the stuff of "the Sunday spirit-screen," but the tricky thing is to hear what the lines are actually saying. They don't all speak for Dickey, a former football star at Clemson. The boy in the poem, sobbing into his jersey, is drawn by Norman Rockwell, whose art of half-truths misses life's bleakness, so stints on its glory. Dickey sees how the glory is contingent on loss. Not all of us win; on the contrary, everybody loses. Once golden like the poet, in his fantasy life a dead ringer for Paul Hornung, the Packers' great running back, we subside into gray middle age. The poem's last lines tell us, when we look at them again, that we and the dying man are going the same way. Forever. But this isn't a poem that sets up expectations only to overthrow them, and the emotion it brims with is real.

Football gives Dickey his taking-off point for considering some home truths, incident to living. Life hangs by a hair, but the bruises it prints on us, "as from/ Scrimmage with the varsity," are man-creating and help us survive. "The Bee," dedicated to the football coaches of Clemson, acts out this proposition and is meanwhile an ode to the game. Putting the old wingback through his paces again, knee action high as it was in his youth, fat man's body exploding through the five-hole over tackle, it bids him dig hard, for something must be saved. His son, stung by a bee that won't let him go, is running in panic into the murderous traffic of the highway. Racing to save him, the poet hears his dead coaches, their voices still quick on the air. "Get the lead out," they scream, and Dickey, leaving his feet at the last possible moment, brings his son down "where/ He lives." At the end of this marvelous poem, he salutes the dead instructor who taught him: "Coach Norton, I am your boy."

But no modern poet is easier to poke fun at. More about football, "In the Pocket" is fun, except that the joke is on him. In the grasp of pursuers—"enemies," he calls them—he reaches inside himself, as sports writers say:

> hit move scramble
> Before death and the ground
> Come up LEAP STAND KILL DIE STRIKE
> Now.

That is what the writers mean when they liken football to life, and the only possible response is dismay. Dickey had genius, many poems attesting it, but critical talent wasn't his. He wrote too much, twenty volumes in thirty years, and the failures he left unchallenged drag his large output earthwards.

He has a sappy portentous side, and his young man's silliness doesn't go away. In prose reflections (*Sorties*) he should have kept to himself, he considers masturbation, "one of the most profound forms of self-communication." The best "abdominal exercise" was fucking. His wrinkled skin prompts this observation: "You can look at your foot... and it is not the foot you ever had before." Well, yes. In his late forties, he wondered how he would spend the rest of his life. A whirlwind, it was. "But is it the *right* whirlwind?" He goes on about sex, but "phantom women of the mind" got to him more than real ones. The confusion introduces a wistful Platonist, one who believes (according to Robert Frost) that "what we have here is an imperfect copy of what is in heaven. The woman you have is an imperfect copy of some woman in heaven or in someone else's bed." That is Dickey's idea. For better or worse, his poetry is restless, always looking over the fence. I'll come to the better part of this later.

He offers a target as broad as a barn, and critics who don't like him have a field day. He wouldn't keep his head down. That made him highly vulnerable, said Monroe Spears, a sympathetic critic. But this was lucky, for without the vulnerability, good things in his poetry wouldn't happen. In his novel *Deliverance* he is Lewis, he told himself, a great white hunter more talkative than Hemingway's. His ideal society is peopled by "survivors" who live in the woods, hunting, fishing, and strumming guitars. Surprising us, Dickey had the nerve to sneer at Robert Bly. But I vote Yes to the novel's big idea. Thinking of how it would be in the wild, the hero says: "You'd die early, and you'd suffer, and your children would suffer, but you'd be in touch."

The nature lover owed a lot to art. Evaluating an artist friend ("somewhat derivative"), he draws his own portrait, ecstatic as he bends to the work. Surely, some "original inscape" must be coming. "Instead, when it comes, it comes out looking like Graham Sutherland or Van Gogh." "Inscape" is a tip-off, and much of him comes out like Hopkins, "hoe blade buckle bifocal," and so on. His

first-person pronoun harks back to Whitman's, and trying out the
high rhetorical wire, he tilts toward Hart Crane: "O claspable/ Symbol the unforeseen on home ground The thing that sustains us forever" ("Coming Back to America"). Dylan Thomas was one of his
heroes, "the only predecessor." These are dangerous masters.

He isn't a discursive poet, his unit being the line, not the verse
paragraph. Many lines are catena, multicolored beads on a string.
In "The Shark's Parlor":

> crabs scuttling from under the floor...
> An almighty fin in trouble
> a moiling of secret forces a false start
> Of water a round wave growing.

His limitation shows vividly if you put him with a great blank verse
poet like Stevens. "Sunday Morning" and "Le Monocle de Mon
Oncle" harness the mind. That isn't where Dickey lives.

His apprehension of things is paratactic, circumscribing what he
can do. A psychologist like him finds it hard to sustain interest, and
his long poems gleam only sporadically "like the flashing of a
shield." The phrase, from Wordsworth's *Prelude*, suggests the good
and bad of him. In between the gleams, the matter, as with
Wordsworth, inclines to turgid. But Wordsworth, his strength foiled
by many weaknesses, is still a master of discursive poetry. Partly
this is a function of prosody. His long line, in *The Prelude* and elsewhere, doesn't cobble together shorter lines, like Dickey's in his
"wall of words" poems, but is seamlessly itself. Dave Smith, looking at his MSS in the Washington University Library, St. Louis, saw
how drafts of his "May Day Sermon" seek to create long lines by
collapsing shorter ones. At least he knew what he want of.

But his catena are crystalline, enough of them to compel attention. In "The Escape" they coalesce, creating a structure like the
windowpanes in the poem, fitting the noon sun together:

> An enormous glass-fronted hospital
> Rises across the street, the traffic
> Roars equally from all four sides
> And often, from a textile mill,
> A teen-age girl wanders by,
> Her head in a singing cloth

> Still humming with bobbins and looms.

A figure of Edwin Muir's gives the character and difficulty of poetry like Dickey's: "The windows cast such brightness/ Outwards that none could see what was within." ("Effigies") Turned opaque by the sun reflecting off the glass, they aren't instrumental to meaning but the meaning.

The difficulty isn't the kind that arises from complex meanings but from a built-in liability of oracular poetry. "Dark with excessive bright," it gives priority to effects over causes. Yeats on Hopkins (in the *Oxford Book of Modern Verse*) seems on the point or near it. "His meaning is like some faint sound that strains the ear, comes out of words, passes to and fro between them, goes back into words, his manner a last development of poetical diction." "Poetical diction" means an arresting but florid vocabulary, language disoriented with a view to enhancing perception. Change the content, "never the form," said a cynical English statesman, good advice but Dickey ignores it. Like Hopkins and the other masters he emulates, he defeats expectation in diction and syntax:

> Snakes under the cloud live more
> In their curves to move. Rain falls
> With the instant, conclusive chill
>
> Of a gnat flying into the eye.
> Crows fall to the temple roof;
> An American feels with his shoulders
> Their new flightless weight be born.
>
> > ("Paestum")

The fracturing of normal usage irritates more than enlightens, and seems a modern affectation that will pass.

His self-conscious style approximates the condition of music, the Romantic kind that aims to pin you to the wall. The other side of this is a paucity of nice discriminations. Declaimed poetry grows monotonous, and the bard is a windbag in long poems like "Reincarnation (II)." He hoped for language "which has a kind of unbridled frenzy about it," becoming (as he acknowledged) inevitably more obscure. Like Mark Rothko, to whom he compared himself, he loved colors, "just colors," and wanted to build up "great shimmering walls of words." It seems they went up at command or by magic, like the walls that obeyed Amphion's lyre. His best poems say he knew better but his esthetic is slippery, befitting the man who had been drunk (if you believe him) for the last twenty-five years. This was boasting but of a piece with his advice to his students at Carolina. Tune into the "celestial wireless," he told them, the worst advice you can give to the young.

He wants so much, like a Thomas Wolfe in poetry, and the strain and cupidity tell. Everything is pristine and worth wonder. Compared to frivolous city fellers, he's awfully down to earth. In poetry, it's "the real, deep thing" that engages him, and he is "sure sick to death" of literary sophists. No misguided Platonist (the moralist now, not the lover of ideal women) put more stress on content, a great poem's "first prerequisite." Of course he didn't cotton to Berryman, all that intolerable *playing* (his italics). Eliot's subtleties went by him, and his having-us-on definition of poetry as "superior amusement" was like a red flag to his bull. To forfeit this side of poetry and/ or Eliot's breezy view of it seems too bad, a loss for poetry in general, in particular Dickey's.

"Learned treatises" on poetry made his skin prickle, like learned poetry, Eliot's or Pound's. He said "intelligence always leads to overrefinement," and against "palaver, and analysis" posed "large basic emotions." I think we take his point while deploring its tendency. Our age of criticism has had its revenge on a poet who looked skeptically at academic critics, pecking away at their laptops. Being a critic, I have a laptop, but have had to lean on a friend who knows how to "access" the library's outsize computer. Punching up the poet's name, my friend makes learned titles appear on the screen, in this case of Dickey, upwards of 300. Though he was vain enough, that would have appalled him.

\* \* \*

But what he said about Robinson Jeffers holds for him too. His poems "carry the day despite everything." Poetry struck him with the force of revelation, and he never got off the road to Damascus. Reading Theodore Roethke, "the greatest poet this country has yet produced," he realized with astonishment that he wasn't dead. Hyperbole is his element, but the second term at least is true, his poetry bearing it out. One way or another he wriggled free of mortality, getting beyond himself or outside himself. When he pronounces on life, his voice seems to know something he didn't.

In his "May Day Sermon," he brings us to the place where God speaks from the burning bush:

> About nakedness: understand how butterflies, amazed, pass
>    out
> Of their natal silks how the tight snake takes a great
>    breath bursts
> Through himself and leaves himself behind how a man casts
>    finally
> Off everything that shields him from another beholds his
>    loins
> Shine with his children forever burn with the very juice
> Of resurrection: such shining is how the spring creek comes
> Forth from its sunken rocks it is how the trout foams and
>    turns on
> Himself heads upstream, breathing mist like water, for the
>    cold
> Mountain of his birth.

Thanks to an enabling poet, down-and-outers, not out of pocket but evacuated in spirit, burst through the imprisoning bounds of the city into a bed of roses ("Bums, on Waking"). If we say that poetry is an act of generosity, Dickey's illustrates what this means.

He sought to re-create the world, and oxymoron, the conceit of the contraries, is a means to his end. "I want to work with extremely crazy, apparently unjustifiable juxtapositions," he said, opening as great a division as possible between his comparative terms. Sometimes he fails to bridge them or is only showing off. When this happens, he is like Icarus falling into the sea, a failure but the splash makes you notice. Napalm and high-octane fuel pair with good bourbon and GI juice in "The Firebombing," and the plane carries a monstrous burden "under the undeodorized arms" of its wings. I'd rate these pairings only so-so. In "Power and Light," however, he straps crampons on his shoes to climb the basement stairs, smiling when he says this, an improvement.

All poets are oxymoronic, and really good poets make ill-assorted things complicitous. Seeing them together, we don't find strangeness but congruity we hadn't noticed before. Montale, a modern master—Dickey does variations on him in his "Free-Flight Improvisations"—has an antipoetic sun like drippings on chimney tops, and iridescent words like the scales on a dying mullet. Many grudge this mordant phrasing but he wills us to endorse it, right for the milieu he works in. Reshuffling old bones, Dickey is like that.

But though he shares Montale's linguistic idiosyncrasies, adjusting standard grammar and the way words reticulate, these two poets in essentials are apples and oranges. Dickey's poetry is old fashioned, an honorable word, and in its attitudes toward life more pro than anti. A juster comparison is with Robinson Jeffers, who deplored most modern poetry in English as anti-life or defeatist. It gave up its body, meaning both content and conventional form, trying to save its soul. For Jeffers and Dickey, saving the soul involved reclamation work, in the case of Jeffers a return to narrative poetry, in Dickey's to the "old Shakespeherian rag."

His poetry struts its stuff, frowned on by approved moderns, Eliot, his great antagonist, heading the list. Whatever the subject, it lights up "Like a bonfire seen through an eyelid" ("A Folk Singer of the Thirties"). The eyelid is the delimiting form. A poem for a dying lady, "Angina" is highly formal—try counting the beats per line and estimating the kind of poetic foot your ear seems to be hearing. Emotion that might be mawkish wells up in this poem, but the controlling form makes it supportable. What do we think of when we think of love? Dickey's poet thinks of taking a chairlift

> Up a staircase burning with dust
> In the afternoon sun slanted also
> Like stairs without steps
> To a room where an old woman lies.

From the pink radio comes helplessly bad music, her only help. And death,

> A chastened, respectful presence
> Forced by years of excessive quiet
> To be stiller than wallpaper roses,
>
> Waits, twined in the roses, saying slowly
> To itself, as sprier and sprier
> Generations of disc jockeys chatter,
> I must be still and not worry,
> Not worry, not worry, to hold
> My peace, my poor place, my own.

Macabre and tender, this ending is like Dickinson a hundred years later, not least in reclaiming her spareness of line.

Conceiving of poetry as "part of the Heraclitean flux," Dickey, not thinking hard enough, rejected "marmoreal, closed forms." Pope is no doubt marmoreal, and so are epigrammatists like Landor. But all form is closed, decisions having been taken, and this sounds suspiciously modern, worse yet, post-modern. Still, he jibbed at the role assigned him, "a kind of spokesman for spontaneity," and said "nothing can exist without form." His distinguishing thing—after you notice the sensibility, vigor, knack for invention, etc.—is that he is a formalist in an age of slapdash. His style is gerundival (moving/ unfurling/ keeping/ covering/ living/ watching), and favors parallel constructions:

> In some guise or another he is near them when they are
>     weeping without sound
> When the teen-age son has quit school when the girl has
>     broken up

With the basketball star when the banker walks out on his wife. (Both quotations from "The Fiend," a.k.a. The Poet.) Whitman, famous for breaking the mold, is such another, both needing a centripetal pull.

Or the pull is away from the ego. Too much "I" is a problem in Dickey, and knowing that, he took measures. He didn't want to be the failed writer of "The Zodiac" who "can't get rid of himself enough/ To write poetry." He gets rid of himself by hitching on to public events (like the inaugural of the president or the governor of South Carolina), or by preferring narrative forms to lyric, where the danger of drenching the poem in the self is much greater. "The Eye-Beaters" tells a story, glossed in the margins à la "The Ancient Mariner," and "Falling," taking off from a clipping in the *Times*, reclaims territory that used to be fiction's. Doing what he can to slough the tyranny of self, he imagines his way into a woman's life, or joins his voice to other voices, one a Chinese poet's who died more than a millennium before him. "The dead at their work-bench altars" tutor his ego, letting him know there's nothing new beneath the sun.

One of his permanent poems, "The Rain Guitar," shows the opportunist, always a good role for a poet. Traveling England in the rain, he has his guitar with him, and it prompts the question: "With what I had, what could I do?" Winchester is the scene, but where is the cathedral? "Out of sight, but somewhere around," like the War in the Pacific, North Georgia railroad track, British marching songs, and a buck dance. Harmonizing, they make a tune all its own, affecting, also comic, also "improved"—Dickey's word—by lumping discrete things together, then fishing for a common term.

He has a gift for comedy, seen to best advantage in "Daughter." Powerful stuff comes our way in this poem—"Roll, real God. Roll through us"—and we might end up stranded in the land of rodomontade. But humor, toning things down, retrieves them. Its function is more than expedient, however, true of all the great comic turns, beginning with the Drunken Porter in *Macbeth*. Not chastely classical but deliberately impure, Dickey mixes tears and laughter, making a compound tougher than its unadulterated parts.

A poet in the modern idiom, he mostly frees himself of old constraints like rhyme and meter. But no good verse is free, an invidious word for poetry, and conventional forms are vestigial in him, like the ghost of iambic pentameter in *The Waste Land*. He likes writing in stanzas, for example septets:

> And now the green household is dark.
> The half-moon completely is shining
> On the earth-lighted tops of the trees.
> To be dead, a house must be still.
> The floor and the walls wave me slowly;
> I am deep in them over my head.
> The needles and pine cones about me.
> ("In the Tree House at Night")

This sounds to my ear like a sestina, structure being firmly linear, and feeling intensely focused, at the same time dispersed. Each stanza—there are eight altogether—walls itself off from the others, and such unity as you get comes from the anapestic rhythm, Dickey's hallmark. After seven lines, his poem wants to break off, but the beat, impelling us forward, won't let it.

He feels at home in short lines, and if his metric were old-style, it would often be trimeter. The short line suits and helps generate his uncomplicated truths, simple but not simple minded. Familiar protagonists keep turning up, as in a repertory theater: stone cutters, hunters, fishermen, soldiers and aviators, men of action, not intro-spection. "Therapist, farewell," he says in "The Eye-Beaters." "Give me my spear." Don't call him "macho," however, but a man who has his hands on the ropes. His competent heroes reflect him. "I have had my time," he says in "Summer," and we believe it.

"The Lifeguard," stamped with the seal of the Norton Anthol-ogy, is a tale of balked purpose and young life cut short, but an emphatic rhythm, both at ease and powerful, asserts continuities. Words recur, half a dozen of them, as in a sestina, and feminine endings heighten the disciplined run of the lines. At the end of each six-line stanza, exhaustion supervenes, the three-beat line reducing to two, and the poem seems to die on us. But then, a breath taken, it gets going again. This isn't dogged or defiant, like Beckett's "I can't go on, I'll go on," only natural, the way spring follows winter.

Form is the hero in "Fence Wire," from *Helmets*, the volume where Dickey comes into his own. "Arranging" the fenced-in acres of a farm, the humming sound of electric current defines the life of its animals too. It does this the way Stevens' jar on a hill in Tennessee takes dominion over the world that surrounds it. A war poem, "Horses and Prisoners," from the same volume, has a figure that suggests Dickey's special achievement, formal but incandescent. Growing flowers pound like hooves in the grassy infield where the horses used to be, and the dead men are enclosed by the poet's mind, "a fence on fire."

His commitment to form isn't generally acknowledged. Howard Nemerov in a 1963 review of *Drowning with Others*, sees "a willed mysticism," damaging, if true. Nemerov's poet wills himself "to sink out of sight," like the man who speaks in "The Driver," elud-ing the shape (or form) that declares him. But this version of Dickey misses the mark. Form in his poetry is the condition of life, and the "fence," always there, prevents it from leaking away.

Two poems worth going back to clarify his conservatism, the kind that holds fast to dear life. In "The Driver," he swims down to a submerged half-track and sits where the dead driver of the title sat before him. Wanting to cross over to the undiscovered country, he says or tries to say: "I am become pure spirit." But only the dead, who no longer hear life's high requiem, can say that. At last he swims back to the surface, and leaping for the sky just before dark-ness claims him, fills his lungs with the breath of life.

Opting for life, he opts for a purview of truth. Religious cranks and political ideologues are avid of the whole truth, like willfully mystic poets. First, though, they have to kill their truth, impaling it like a specimen. No poet aspires more than Dickey, but he settles for our human condition, necessarily a privation. This happens again in "A Dog Sleeping on My Feet." Taking his cue from the sleeping animal, he yearns to speak "The hypnotized language of beasts." This may be worth doing but doesn't go with what we are, and at last he breaks off, faltering and failing "Back into the human tongue."

"Camden Town" is his "Ode to a Nightingale." A poem of Flight-Sleep, he called it, sleep like the easeful death he is half in love with. But death entails annihilation, "to thy high requiem become a sod," and the man in the cockpit reasserts control. His goggles blaze with darkness as he turns back to life, wrenching the compass "from its dream/ Of all the West."

The yearning to put off the intelligent self, always there in the poetry, energizes what it might vitiate, were the poet's hand less sure. Here are some poems that register the assurance. "Autumn," a short-lines poem (unrhymed triplets), says how we shall all be changed when the angel of renewal descends into Hell, and breathing upon grass roots, delivers the year from its thinking to "the mindless one color of life." In "The Heaven of Animals," a poem like and unlike Isaiah, hunter and hunted, the killer and the one who is killed, don't deny what they are but hone it to perfection, living together in "a sovereign floating of joy." A small boy's imagination, as it might be a poet's, evokes the a-rational world of boyhood in "Pursuit from Under." And in "False Youth Autumn 11 Clothes of the Age," the dear God of the wildness of poetry is before us:

> Disintegrating, his one eye raveling
> Out, filthy strings flying
> From the white feathers, one wing nearly gone:
> Blind eagle but flying
> Where I walk...
> And get a lifetime look at my bird's
> One word, raggedly blazing with extinction and soaring
> loose
> In red threads burning up white until I am shot in the back
> Through my wings   or ripped apart
> For rags:
> *Poetry.*

In the Wolverine poem I began with, Dickey seems to exalt a "mindless" way of being, and it wouldn't be hard to fellow this example with others. But it isn't intellect he takes aim at. The butt of his wrath is the desiccated man who tries decapitation. John Crowe Ransom saw him at it in his poem, "Painted Head," where the mind, floating free, leaves "the body bush" behind. Dickey's poems explore what happens when the mind is independent of the body. Finding out what this is, he quit his advertising job, sold his house, and headed for the territories.

"The Salt Marsh," another keeper from the volume Nemerov looked at, locates him amid stalks of sawgrass, swallowed up in a growing field that offers no promise of harvest. His body tingles like salt crystals, and the sun directly above him destroys all four points of the compass. But losing himself he finds himself, and as the grass bends before the wind, he bends with it. "Supple" is the word for this, for the poetry too, not stately but quick with motion, often musical, and by its nature communicating repose.

Music isn't prized much in modern poetry, going all the way back to Pound's animadversions on the "swishiness and slushiness" of the post-Swinburnian line. Poets and their critics, canonizing anti-poetry, equate dissonance and truth, and the bulk of Montale will illustrate nicely. Music resonates in Dickey, though, setting him apart in his time. He knew what poetry ought to offer, not finding it in Charles Olson, dismissed for his lack of "personal rhythm," or in William Carlos Williams' "tiresome and predictable prosiness," still less in Mark Strand, whose "deliberate eccentricity" seemed merely silly. Never mind if these judgments meet your agreement: all the words are chosen with malice aforethought. Thinking them over gets you closer to Dickey's intention.

The rhythm he heard had to be "characteristic of the writer." Also it had to be syncopated, i.e., off the beat. His ear is cocked for the beat, however, absolutely the sine qua non. The critical thing was to *move* on the song without losing the music. In the *Buckdancer* poems, the key changes often, but not so often that it baffles the ear. Prosiness was tameness, when the poem stops swinging or its claws are blunted or drawn.

The "timid poem" needed wildness, Dickey said in his Wolverine poem. But he wasn't a primitive, flinging about the bedclothes

or burning down the house, and his lines for Richard Wilbur declare an un-Beat-like poet:

> the great wild thing is not seeing
> All the way in to the center,
> But holding yourself at the edge,
> Alive, where one can get a look.

"Holding yourself," as if walking a tightrope: this poet is poised,
like a bow-and-arrow man, like a musician, two roles Dickey excelled in. The other term to key on is "alive," evidently equated
with wildness. It doesn't mean abandon, though, but the abandon-
ing of self that goes with complete involvement. The hero in the
novel makes this meaning vivid.

Writing about writers, especially poets, one tends to straighten
them out, a mistake. I mustn't discover too much order in Dickey,
who had his crazy side, like Ancient Pistol when he sang of Africa
and golden joys. The wildness he commends to us is partly itself,
hair-raising when it gets into the music. Some examples:

> on August week ends the cold of a personal ice age
> Comes up through my bare feet.
>                                              ("Pursuit from Under")

> My life belongs to the world. I will do what I can.
>                                              ("The Strength of Fields")

Or this reminiscence of an old man in a terminal ward, lying back,

> his eyes filmed, unappeased,
> As all of them, clucking, pillow-patting,
> Come to help his best savagery blaze, doomed, dead-
> game, demanding, unreasonably
> Battling to the death for what is his.
>                                              ("Gamecock")

This recognizable voice of Dickey's sounds in an early poem,
"The Performance," remembering Donald Armstrong, a fellow air-
man, beheaded by the Japanese. About to die, he rises, kingly, round-
shouldered, then kneels

down in himself
Beside his hacked, glittering grave, having done
All things in this life that he could.

That is the voice we want in poetry, suitable for life's occasions, the kind we must get through alone.

# Index